THE POWER OF RESTORATIVE JUSTICE

Healing Dialogues

Dr. Maxwell Shimba

Shimba Publishing, LLC.

Printed in the United States of America

TABLE OF CONTENTS

INTRODUCTION

The Philosophy of Restorative Justice

Restorative justice represents a paradigm shift from traditional punitive justice systems to approaches focused on healing, rehabilitation, and reintegration. Unlike conventional systems that prioritize punishment, restorative justice seeks to repair harm, restore relationships, and build community resilience. At its core, restorative justice views crime not merely as a violation of law but as an offense against individuals and the community.

Historical Context and Evolution

The roots of restorative justice can be traced back to ancient and indigenous practices across various cultures. These early systems emphasized reconciliation, restitution, and the collective well-being of the community. For example, Indigenous peoples of North America, the Maori of New Zealand, and various African communities historically practiced forms of justice that focused on healing and restoring harmony.

In the 1970s, the modern restorative justice movement began to take shape in the Western world. Scholars and practitioners started to challenge the prevailing punitive approaches, advocating for systems that addressed the needs of victims, offenders, and the community. This movement was influenced by increasing dissatisfaction with the high rates of recidivism and the negative impacts of incarceration on individuals and communities.

Objectives and Principles of Victim-Offender Mediation

Victim-offender mediation is a pivotal process within the restorative justice framework. Its primary objectives include:

- Providing a safe space for victims to express their experiences and needs.

- Encouraging offenders to take responsibility for their actions and understand the impact on victims.

- Facilitating dialogue and mutual understanding between victims and offenders.

- Developing mutually agreed-upon plans for restitution and reparation.

- Promoting healing, forgiveness, and reintegration of both victims and offenders into the community.

Victim-offender mediation is built on several core principles:

1. Repairing Harm: The primary goal is to address the harm caused by the crime and find ways to make amends.

2. Voluntary Participation: Both victims and offenders participate voluntarily, ensuring that the process is consensual and respectful.

3. Inclusive Dialogue: The process encourages open and honest communication, allowing all parties to express their perspectives and feelings.

4. Accountability: Offenders are encouraged to take responsibility for their actions and make amends to those they have harmed.

5. Empowerment: Victims are given a voice and an active role in the justice process, promoting their healing and empowerment.

The Scope of This Book

This book aims to provide a comprehensive understanding of restorative justice and victim-offender mediation. It will explore the philosophy, principles, and practices of restorative justice, offering insights into its transformative potential. Through theoretical discussions, practical guidance, and real-world examples, readers will gain a deeper appreciation of how restorative justice can repair harm, restore relationships, and build resilient communities.

Structure of the Book

The book is structured into several chapters, each focusing on different aspects of restorative justice and victim-offender mediation:

1. Understanding Restorative Justice: This chapter provides an overview of restorative justice, comparing it with traditional justice systems and highlighting its key stakeholders.

2. The Process of Victim-Offender Mediation: This chapter delves into the steps involved in victim-offender mediation, from preparation and assessment to the facilitation of mediation sessions and follow-up.

3. Benefits of Victim-Offender Mediation: This chapter explores the various benefits of mediation for victims, offenders, and communities.

4. The Role of Mediators: This chapter discusses the qualifications, skills, and ethical considerations for mediators.

5. Case Studies in Victim-Offender Mediation: This chapter presents success stories and critical analyses of mediation cases.

6. Psychological and Emotional Impact: This chapter examines the psychological and emotional effects of mediation on participants.

7. Legal and Policy Frameworks: This chapter explores how mediation can be integrated into legal systems and the necessary policy support.

8. Cultural Sensitivity in Mediation: This chapter addresses the importance of cultural sensitivity and provides examples from various cultures.

9. Training and Education for Practitioners: This chapter outlines the training and education required for restorative justice practitioners.

10. Challenges and Criticisms: This chapter discusses the challenges and criticisms of restorative justice and offers strategies for addressing them.

11. Future Directions in Restorative Justice: This chapter looks at innovations and future directions for restorative justice practice.

Call to Action

Restorative justice presents an opportunity to rethink and reshape our responses to crime and conflict. By embracing restorative practices, we can create a justice system that prioritizes healing, accountability, and community resilience. This book invites readers—whether they are practitioners, policymakers, or community members—to explore the principles and practices of restorative justice and consider how they can contribute to a more just and compassionate society.

Conclusion

The introduction to restorative justice and victim-offender mediation sets the stage for a deeper exploration of this transformative approach to justice. By shifting the focus from punishment to healing, restorative justice offers a path toward reconciliation and resilience. This book aims to equip readers with the knowledge and tools needed to understand, implement, and advocate for restorative justice in their communities.

Historical Context and Evolution

The roots of restorative justice can be traced back to indigenous practices and ancient traditions across various cultures. These early systems emphasized reconciliation, restitution, and the collective well-being of the community, prioritizing the repair of relationships over punishment. By focusing on healing and community cohesion, these traditional forms of justice sought to address the harm caused by wrongdoing in ways that benefited both the individual and the group.

Indigenous Practices

Many indigenous cultures around the world practiced forms of restorative justice long before the concept was formalized in modern legal systems. For example, the Native American tribes in North America employed peacemaking circles, where community members, including the victim and the offender, gathered to discuss the harm done and how to repair it. The process was deeply rooted in the community's values and traditions, emphasizing dialogue, mutual respect, and consensus.

Similarly, the Maori people of New Zealand used a process known as "whanau" or family conferencing, where extended family members participated in resolving conflicts and addressing wrongdoing. This approach highlighted the importance of collective responsibility and the reintegration of the offender into the community.

Ancient Traditions

Ancient legal systems, such as those in Mesopotamia, ancient Greece, and early medieval Europe, also incorporated restorative elements. The Code of Hammurabi, one of the oldest known legal codes, included provisions for restitution, where offenders were required to compensate victims for their losses. In ancient Greece, practices such as "diaitēsis" involved mediators helping parties reach an agreement on compensation for wrongs committed.

In medieval Europe, practices like "wergild" in Anglo-Saxon law allowed for the payment of compensation to victims or their families, reflecting a restorative approach to justice. These traditions underscored the principle that justice should restore balance and address the needs of those harmed.

Modern Restorative Justice Movement

The modern restorative justice movement began to take shape in the 1970s, initially as a response to the limitations and failures of the punitive justice system. Scholars, practitioners, and community activists began advocating for alternatives that focused on repairing harm and promoting healing. This movement was significantly influenced by the work of criminologists and sociologists who highlighted the benefits of restorative practices.

One of the pioneering programs was the Victim-Offender Reconciliation Program (VORP) in Kitchener, Ontario, Canada, initiated in 1974. This program brought victims and offenders together to discuss the impact of the crime and agree on a plan for restitution. The success of VORP inspired similar programs across North America and Europe.

Institutionalization and Formalization

Over the past few decades, restorative justice has gained momentum, driven by the need for more humane and effective responses to crime. Countries around the world have incorporated restorative practices into their legal systems. For example, in New Zealand, the 1989 Children, Young Persons, and Their Families Act mandated the use of family group conferences for young offenders, making restorative justice a central part of the juvenile justice system.

In South Africa, the Truth and Reconciliation Commission (TRC), established in 1995, used restorative principles to address the atrocities committed during apartheid. The TRC provided a platform for victims to share their stories and for perpetrators to confess their crimes, promoting national healing and reconciliation.

Contemporary Developments

Today, restorative justice continues to evolve and expand its reach. It is used not only in criminal justice but also in schools, workplaces, and communities to address conflicts and foster a culture of empathy and accountability. Restorative justice practices are being integrated into various levels of the legal system, from juvenile justice programs to adult criminal courts.

Internationally, organizations like the United Nations have recognized and promoted restorative justice as a valuable tool for addressing crime and conflict. The UN's Basic Principles on the Use of Restorative Justice Programmes in Criminal Matters, adopted in 2002, provides guidelines for the implementation of restorative justice practices worldwide.

Conclusion

The historical context and evolution of restorative justice reveal its deep roots in human traditions and its potential for addressing harm in meaningful ways. From ancient practices of restitution to modern-day reconciliation programs, restorative justice offers a framework for repairing relationships and strengthening communities. As this movement continues to grow and adapt, it provides a hopeful vision for a more just and compassionate society.

Objectives and Principles of Victim-Offender Mediation

Victim-offender mediation is a pivotal process within the restorative justice framework, aimed at addressing the harm caused by criminal behavior and fostering healing and reconciliation. The primary objectives of victim-offender mediation include:

Providing a Safe Space for Victims to Express Their Experiences and Needs

One of the foremost objectives of victim-offender mediation is to create a safe and supportive environment where victims can freely express their experiences, emotions, and needs. Traditional justice systems often overlook the personal impact of crime on victims, focusing instead on legal procedures and outcomes. In contrast, restorative justice centers the victim's voice, acknowledging their pain and validating their experiences. This safe space allows victims to share how the crime has affected them, which can be a crucial step in their healing process.

Encouraging Offenders to Take Responsibility

Another key objective of victim-offender mediation is to encourage offenders to take responsibility for their actions. This involves more than just admitting guilt; it requires offenders to understand the impact of their behavior on the victims and the community. Through the mediation process, offenders are guided to recognize the harm they have caused and to express remorse. This acknowledgment can be a powerful catalyst for personal growth and rehabilitation, as it prompts offenders to reflect on their actions and commit to making amends.

Facilitating Dialogue and Mutual Understanding

Victim-offender mediation facilitates open and honest dialogue between victims and offenders. This dialogue is structured and guided by a trained mediator who ensures that the conversation remains respectful and constructive. The goal is to foster mutual understanding, allowing both parties to see the situation from each other's perspectives. This can lead to a greater sense of empathy and reduce feelings of anger and resentment. By understanding the context and motivations behind the offense, victims may find it easier to forgive, and offenders may gain insights that prevent future wrongdoing.

Developing Mutually Agreed-Upon Plans for Restitution and Reparation

A central component of victim-offender mediation is the development of mutually agreed-upon plans for restitution and reparation. This process involves collaborative problem-solving, where both victims and offenders work together to identify ways to repair the harm caused by the crime. Restitution can take many forms, including financial compensation, community service, or personal acts of reparation. The aim is to restore the balance disrupted by the offense and to provide a tangible means for offenders to make amends. These agreements are crafted with the input and consent of both parties, ensuring that the solutions are fair and meaningful.

Promoting Healing, Forgiveness, and Reintegration

The ultimate objective of victim-offender mediation is to promote healing, forgiveness, and the reintegration of both victims and offenders into the community. Healing for victims involves not only receiving compensation for their losses but also finding emotional closure and moving forward with their lives. For offenders, healing means taking responsibility, making amends, and reintegrating into society as productive and accountable members. The process of mediation can also foster forgiveness, as victims and offenders engage in a dialogue that humanizes both parties and builds bridges of understanding. Reintegration is supported by the community's involvement and the ongoing support provided to both victims and offenders as they navigate their paths to recovery.

Principles of Victim-Offender Mediation

Victim-offender mediation is guided by several core principles that ensure the process is ethical, effective, and centered on the needs of those involved:

Voluntary Participation

Participation in victim-offender mediation is entirely voluntary for both victims and offenders. This principle is crucial to the integrity of the process, as it ensures that all parties are genuinely willing to engage in dialogue and seek resolution. Coercion or pressure to participate undermines the authenticity and potential outcomes of the mediation.

Respect and Dignity

The mediation process is conducted with the utmost respect and dignity for all participants. This includes respecting the experiences, emotions, and perspectives of both victims and offenders. Mediators are trained to create an environment that honors the humanity of each person involved, fostering a space where healing and reconciliation can occur.

Confidentiality

Confidentiality is a cornerstone of victim-offender mediation. The details of the discussions and the agreements reached are kept private, providing a safe space for open and honest communication. This confidentiality encourages participants to speak freely and to address the issues at the heart of the conflict without fear of external judgment or repercussions.

Empowerment

Victim-offender mediation seeks to empower both victims and offenders. For victims, this means having a voice in the justice process and actively participating in the resolution of the harm caused. For offenders, empowerment comes from taking responsibility for their actions and engaging in meaningful acts of reparation. This empowerment fosters a sense of agency and ownership over the outcomes.

Collaboration

The mediation process is inherently collaborative, involving the active participation of both victims and offenders in developing solutions. This collaborative approach ensures that the resolutions are tailored to the specific needs and circumstances of those involved, making them more likely to be effective and sustainable.

Accountability

Accountability is a key principle of victim-offender mediation. Offenders are held accountable for their actions in a way that promotes understanding and responsibility. This accountability is not about punishment but about recognizing the impact of one's actions and making amends in a constructive and restorative manner.

Conclusion

Victim-offender mediation is a transformative process that addresses the harm caused by criminal behavior through dialogue, mutual understanding, and collaborative problem-solving. By providing a safe space for victims to express their experiences, encouraging offenders to take responsibility, and developing plans for restitution and reparation, mediation promotes healing, forgiveness, and reintegration. Guided by principles of voluntary participation, respect, confidentiality, empowerment, collaboration, and accountability, victim-offender mediation offers a humane and effective alternative to traditional punitive justice systems.

DR. MAXWELL SHIMBA

CHAPTER 01

UNDERSTANDING RESTORATIVE JUSTICE

Definition and Core Concepts

Restorative justice is an approach to justice that emphasizes the repair of harm caused by criminal behavior. Unlike traditional punitive justice systems, which focus on punishment and deterrence, restorative justice seeks to address the needs of victims, offenders, and the community through inclusive processes that engage all stakeholders in dialogue and decision-making. This chapter explores the definition of restorative justice and its core concepts, providing a foundation for understanding how this transformative approach operates.

Definition of Restorative Justice

Restorative justice is a holistic approach that seeks to heal the wounds caused by crime. It is based on the principle that crime harms people and relationships, and justice should aim to repair that harm. Restorative justice involves all those affected by a crime—the victim, the offender, and the community—in a process that encourages accountability, restitution, and reconciliation.

Key elements of restorative justice include:

1. Involvement of All Stakeholders: Restorative justice actively involves victims, offenders, and community members in the justice process. This participation ensures that the needs and perspectives of all affected parties are considered.

2. Focus on Harm: The approach centers on the harm caused by criminal behavior, rather than on the violation of laws. This shift in focus allows for a more personalized and empathetic response to crime.

3. Repair and Restoration: The primary goal is to repair the harm and restore relationships. This can involve various forms of restitution, including apologies, compensation, community service, and other acts of reparation.

4. Accountability and Responsibility: Offenders are encouraged to take responsibility for their actions and to understand the impact of their behavior on others. This accountability is a crucial step toward rehabilitation and reintegration.

Core Concepts of Restorative Justice

The core concepts of restorative justice provide the framework for its practices and processes. These concepts include accountability, reparation, and reintegration, each of which plays a vital role in achieving the goals of restorative justice.

Accountability

Accountability is a fundamental concept in restorative justice. It involves offenders acknowledging their wrongdoing and understanding the impact of their actions on victims and the community. This process of accountability goes beyond mere admission of guilt; it requires offenders to engage in self-reflection and to recognize the harm they have caused.

In a restorative justice context, accountability is not about imposing punishment but about encouraging offenders to take responsibility. This can involve:

- Participating in Mediation: Offenders may engage in dialogue with victims to hear firsthand how their actions have affected others.

- Making Amends: Offenders may be required to make restitution to victims, which could involve financial compensation, community service, or other reparative actions.

- Reflecting on Behavior: Offenders are encouraged to reflect on the underlying causes of their behavior and to commit to making positive changes.

Reparation

Reparation is the act of making amends for the harm caused by criminal behavior. It is a core concept of restorative justice that focuses on addressing the needs of victims and restoring the balance disrupted by crime. Reparation can take various forms, depending on the nature of the harm and the needs of the victim.

Forms of reparation include:

- Financial Compensation: Offenders may provide financial restitution to victims for any losses or damages incurred.

- Apologies and Acknowledgments: Offenders may offer sincere apologies and acknowledge the impact of their actions on victims and the community.

- Community Service: Offenders may engage in community service projects that benefit the community and demonstrate their commitment to making amends.

- Direct Acts of Reparation: Offenders may undertake specific actions requested by victims, such as repairing damaged property or participating in restorative programs.

The process of reparation is collaborative, involving input from victims, offenders, and community members to ensure that the outcomes are meaningful and effective.

Reintegration

Reintegration is the process of restoring offenders to a constructive and responsible role within the community. It recognizes that, for justice to be truly restorative, offenders must be supported in their efforts to reintegrate and lead productive lives.

Key aspects of reintegration include:

- Supportive Measures: Providing offenders with access to counseling, education, job training, and other resources to help them reintegrate successfully.

- Community Involvement: Encouraging community members to support offenders in their reintegration efforts, reducing stigma and promoting acceptance.

- Ongoing Monitoring: Implementing measures to monitor the progress of offenders and to provide continued support as needed.

Reintegration benefits not only the offenders but also the community, as it reduces recidivism and promotes public safety.

Inclusivity and Dialogue

A distinctive feature of restorative justice is its emphasis on inclusivity and dialogue. The process is designed to bring together victims, offenders, and community members in a structured and respectful dialogue. This inclusivity ensures that all voices are heard and that the outcomes reflect the needs and perspectives of everyone involved.

The dialogue process involves:

- Facilitated Meetings: Trained mediators or facilitators guide the dialogue, ensuring that it remains constructive and focused on healing and resolution.

- Open Communication: Participants are encouraged to speak openly and honestly about their experiences, feelings, and needs.

- Collaborative Decision-Making: The process involves collaborative decision-making, where participants work together to develop solutions and agreements that address the harm caused.

Restorative Justice in Practice

Restorative justice practices can take many forms, ranging from victim-offender mediation to community conferencing and restorative circles. These practices share the common goal of addressing harm and fostering healing through inclusive and participatory processes.

Victim-Offender Mediation: This practice involves direct dialogue between victims and offenders, facilitated by a trained mediator. The aim is to provide victims with an opportunity to express their experiences and needs, and for offenders to take responsibility and make amends.

Community Conferencing: Community conferencing brings together a wider group of stakeholders, including victims, offenders, family members, and community representatives. The goal is to address the broader impact of the crime and to develop collective solutions.

Restorative Circles: Restorative circles are a flexible and inclusive practice that can be used in various settings, such as schools, workplaces, and community groups. Participants sit in a circle and engage in facilitated dialogue to address conflicts, repair harm, and build relationships.

The Impact of Restorative Justice

Restorative justice has a profound impact on individuals and communities. For victims, it provides a sense of closure and empowerment, allowing them to participate actively in the justice process. For offenders, it offers a path to accountability and rehabilitation, reducing the likelihood of reoffending. For communities, it promotes social cohesion and resilience, fostering a culture of empathy and support.

Studies have shown that restorative justice can lead to higher levels of victim satisfaction, reduced recidivism rates, and stronger community bonds. By addressing the root causes of crime and focusing on healing and restoration, restorative justice offers a promising alternative to traditional punitive approaches.

Conclusion

Restorative justice represents a transformative approach to justice that prioritizes the needs of victims, offenders, and the community. By focusing on accountability, reparation, and reintegration, it offers a holistic and humane response to crime. Through inclusive processes that engage all stakeholders in dialogue and decision-making, restorative justice seeks to repair harm, restore relationships, and build resilient communities. As we continue to explore and implement restorative justice practices, we move closer to a more just and compassionate society.

Traditional vs. Restorative Justice Systems

Introduction

The justice system plays a crucial role in maintaining social order and addressing criminal behavior. However, different approaches to justice can yield significantly different outcomes. Traditional justice systems and restorative justice systems represent two contrasting paradigms in dealing with crime. Traditional justice systems often prioritize retribution and deterrence, leading to punitive measures that may not address the underlying causes of crime or the needs of those affected. In contrast, restorative justice systems emphasize healing and reconciliation, aiming to restore balance and promote long-term peace. This chapter explores the differences between these two approaches, highlighting their principles, processes, and impacts on individuals and communities.

Traditional Justice Systems

Traditional justice systems, also known as retributive justice systems, are primarily focused on punishment and deterrence. They operate on the principle that crime is a violation of the law and that justice requires the imposition of penalties on offenders. This approach is deeply rooted in historical and legal traditions that emphasize retribution and the maintenance of social order through punitive measures.

Principles of Traditional Justice Systems

1. Retribution: The central principle of traditional justice is retribution. This means that offenders are punished in proportion to the severity of their crimes. The idea is to exact a penalty that reflects the harm done, thus serving as a form of societal vengeance.

2. Deterrence: Traditional justice systems aim to deter crime by imposing penalties that discourage offenders and others from committing similar acts. The threat of punishment is intended to create a fear of legal consequences, thereby reducing criminal behavior.

3. Incarceration: Incarceration is a common form of punishment in traditional justice systems. Offenders are removed from society and placed in prisons as a way to protect the public and punish the individual.

4. Adversarial Process: Traditional justice operates through an adversarial process where the state prosecutes the offender, and the defense represents the accused. The focus is on determining guilt or innocence through a formal legal process.

Processes in Traditional Justice Systems

1. Arrest and Prosecution: When a crime is committed, law enforcement agencies investigate, arrest the suspect, and gather evidence. The case is then handed over to prosecutors who decide whether to bring charges.

2. Trial and Sentencing: The accused goes through a trial where evidence is presented, and a judge or jury determines guilt or innocence. If found guilty, the offender is sentenced to a specific penalty, which could include

imprisonment, fines, probation, or other forms of punishment.

3. Punishment and Incarceration: Offenders serve their sentences as determined by the court. This phase focuses on the execution of the punishment, often involving incarceration in a prison or correctional facility.

Impact of Traditional Justice Systems

While traditional justice systems aim to maintain social order and provide a sense of justice, they often face several criticisms:

- Failure to Address Underlying Causes: Traditional justice systems tend to focus on punishment rather than addressing the root causes of criminal behavior, such as poverty, addiction, or social inequality.

- Neglect of Victim Needs: Victims' needs and experiences are often sidelined in traditional justice processes. The emphasis on punishment leaves little room for victim participation or emotional healing.

- High Recidivism Rates: Punitive measures like incarceration do not always lead to rehabilitation. Many offenders re-offend after being released, leading to high recidivism rates.

- Overcrowded Prisons: The focus on incarceration has led to overcrowded prison systems, which can exacerbate social and economic problems.

Restorative Justice Systems

Restorative justice systems offer an alternative approach that emphasizes healing, reconciliation, and the repair of harm. Instead of focusing solely on punishment, restorative justice seeks to address the needs of victims, offenders, and the community, fostering a collaborative process aimed at restoring balance and promoting long-term peace.

Principles of Restorative Justice Systems

1. Healing and Reparation: The primary goal of restorative justice is to heal the harm caused by crime. This involves making amends to victims, addressing the needs of offenders, and restoring relationships within the community.

2. Accountability: Offenders are encouraged to take responsibility for their actions and understand the impact of their behavior. Accountability is viewed as a pathway to personal growth and rehabilitation.

3. Inclusion and Participation: Restorative justice processes actively involve victims, offenders, and community members. This inclusive approach ensures that all voices are heard and that solutions are collaborative.

4. Reintegration: Restorative justice aims to reintegrate offenders into society as responsible and productive members. This involves providing support and opportunities for rehabilitation and positive change.

Processes in Restorative Justice Systems

1. Victim-Offender Mediation: This process involves direct dialogue between victims and offenders, facilitated by a trained mediator. The goal is to discuss the impact of the crime, address the needs of the victim, and develop a plan for restitution.

2. Restorative Circles: Restorative circles bring together victims, offenders, family members, and community representatives in a facilitated dialogue. Participants share their experiences, express their needs, and collaboratively develop solutions.

3. Community Conferencing: Community conferencing involves a broader group of stakeholders, including victims, offenders, and community members. The focus is on addressing the harm caused by the crime and developing collective agreements for reparation and reintegration.

Impact of Restorative Justice Systems

Restorative justice systems have demonstrated several positive impacts:

- Victim Satisfaction: Victims often report higher levels of satisfaction with restorative justice processes, as they have the opportunity to be heard and to receive meaningful restitution.

- Offender Rehabilitation: Offenders who participate in restorative justice are more likely to understand the impact of their actions and to engage in personal growth and rehabilitation, leading to lower recidivism rates.

- Community Healing: Restorative justice fosters a sense of community by involving all stakeholders in the justice process. This collaborative approach strengthens social bonds and promotes a culture of empathy and support.

- Reduction in Incarceration: By focusing on reparative measures rather than punitive ones, restorative justice can reduce the reliance on incarceration, alleviating the pressures on overcrowded prison systems.

Comparing Traditional and Restorative Justice Systems

Focus and Goals

- Traditional Justice: Focuses on punishment, deterrence, and retribution. The primary goal is to impose penalties that reflect the severity of the crime.

- Restorative Justice: Focuses on healing, reparation, and reintegration. The primary goal is to repair harm and restore relationships.

Process and Participation

- Traditional Justice: Operates through an adversarial process with limited involvement of victims and community members. The focus is on determining guilt and imposing penalties.

- Restorative Justice: Involves inclusive and collaborative processes that actively engage victims, offenders, and community members. The focus is on dialogue, mutual understanding, and developing reparative solutions.

Outcomes and Impact

- Traditional Justice: Often results in punitive measures that do not address the underlying causes of crime or the needs of victims. High recidivism rates and overcrowded prisons are common outcomes.

- Restorative Justice: Promotes healing, accountability, and reintegration. It addresses the needs of all stakeholders and fosters long-term peace and community resilience.

Conclusion

Traditional justice systems and restorative justice systems represent two fundamentally different approaches to addressing crime. While traditional justice focuses on punishment and deterrence, restorative justice emphasizes healing, reparation, and reintegration. By understanding the principles, processes, and impacts of both approaches, we can better appreciate the potential of restorative justice to transform our responses to crime and to build more just and compassionate communities. As we explore and implement restorative justice practices, we move closer to a justice system that truly meets the needs of victims, offenders, and society as a whole.

Key Stakeholders in Restorative Justice

Restorative justice is a collaborative and inclusive approach to addressing harm caused by criminal behavior. It relies on the active participation of various stakeholders, each playing a crucial role in the process. Key stakeholders in restorative justice include victims, offenders, facilitators, community members, and justice professionals. This chapter explores the roles and contributions of these stakeholders, highlighting their importance in creating a holistic and effective restorative justice process.

Victims

Victims are at the heart of the restorative justice process. The primary focus is on addressing their needs, providing them with a voice, and facilitating their healing and empowerment. In traditional justice systems, victims often feel marginalized and disconnected from the proceedings. Restorative justice seeks to rectify this by actively involving victims in the process and ensuring that their perspectives are central to the resolution.

Roles and Contributions of Victims:

1. Sharing Their Experiences: Victims have the opportunity to share their experiences and express how the crime has impacted them. This can be a crucial step in their healing process, as it validates their suffering and allows them to be heard.

2. Expressing Their Needs: Victims can articulate their needs and expectations for restitution and reparation. This input helps shape the outcomes of the restorative justice process, ensuring that the solutions are meaningful and address their specific needs.

3. Participating in Dialogue: Victims engage in dialogue with offenders, facilitated by mediators, to discuss the harm caused and explore ways to repair it. This interaction can foster understanding, empathy, and a sense of closure.

4. Empowerment and Healing: By actively participating in the justice process, victims regain a sense of control and empowerment. This involvement can contribute significantly to their emotional and psychological healing.

Offenders

Offenders play a critical role in restorative justice by taking responsibility for their actions and participating in the process of making amends. Restorative justice views offenders not just as perpetrators of crime but as individuals capable of change and rehabilitation.

Roles and Contributions of Offenders:

1. Acknowledging Responsibility: Offenders are encouraged to acknowledge their wrongdoings and understand the impact of their actions on victims and the community. This acknowledgment is a crucial step toward accountability and personal growth.

2. Engaging in Dialogue: Offenders participate in mediated dialogues with victims to discuss the harm caused and to hear firsthand how their actions have affected others. This interaction can foster empathy and a deeper understanding of the consequences of their behavior.

3. Making Amends: Offenders are involved in developing and implementing plans for restitution and reparation. This can include financial compensation, community service, apologies, or other acts of reparation that address the harm caused.

4. Rehabilitation and Reintegration: The process supports offenders in their rehabilitation and reintegration

into society. By taking responsibility and making amends, offenders can rebuild trust and work toward becoming productive members of the community.

Facilitators

Facilitators, also known as mediators or restorative justice practitioners, are essential to the restorative justice process. They guide the dialogue, ensure a safe and respectful environment, and help all parties reach mutually agreeable solutions.

Roles and Contributions of Facilitators:

1. Guiding the Process: Facilitators guide the restorative justice process, ensuring that it is structured, fair, and focused on healing and resolution. They create a safe space for dialogue and manage the interactions between participants.

2. Ensuring Inclusivity: Facilitators ensure that all voices are heard and that the process is inclusive. They encourage active participation from victims, offenders, and community members, ensuring that everyone's perspectives are considered.

3. Building Trust: Facilitators build trust among participants by maintaining neutrality, confidentiality, and respect. This trust is crucial for open and honest dialogue and for achieving meaningful outcomes.

4. Developing Agreements: Facilitators assist in developing agreements for restitution and reparation that are acceptable to all parties. They help negotiate and formalize these agreements, ensuring that they are realistic and implementable.

Community Members

Community members play a vital role in restorative justice by providing support, fostering a sense of collective responsibility, and helping to reintegrate both victims and offenders. Their involvement emphasizes the community's role in maintaining social harmony and addressing the broader impacts of crime.

Roles and Contributions of Community Members:

1. Providing Support: Community members provide emotional and practical support to both victims and offenders. This support can be crucial in helping individuals navigate the restorative justice process and in promoting healing.

2. Fostering Collective Responsibility: By participating in restorative justice processes, community members emphasize the importance of collective responsibility for addressing harm and restoring balance. They help create a supportive environment that encourages accountability and reconciliation.

3. Promoting Reintegration: Community members play a key role in the reintegration of offenders. By offering acceptance, opportunities for rehabilitation, and social support, they help offenders rebuild their lives and become responsible members of the community.

4. Enhancing Social Cohesion: The involvement of community members in restorative justice processes fosters social cohesion and resilience. It reinforces the idea that the community is collectively responsible for addressing harm and supporting healing.

Justice Professionals

Justice professionals, including judges, prosecutors, defense attorneys, and law enforcement officers, are integral to the implementation and success of restorative justice. Their support and collaboration are essential for integrating restorative practices into the broader justice system.

Roles and Contributions of Justice Professionals:

1. Supporting Restorative Practices: Justice professionals support the integration of restorative justice practices within the legal system. They advocate for policies and procedures that promote restorative approaches and ensure that cases are referred to restorative justice programs when appropriate.

2. Facilitating Referrals: Judges, prosecutors, and law enforcement officers play a key role in identifying cases suitable for restorative justice and facilitating referrals to restorative programs. Their involvement ensures that restorative justice is considered as a viable option in the justice process.

3. Providing Oversight: Justice professionals provide oversight and ensure that restorative justice processes are conducted fairly and in accordance with legal standards. This oversight helps maintain the integrity and credibility of restorative justice programs.

4. Collaborating with Facilitators: Justice professionals collaborate with facilitators and restorative justice practitioners to ensure that the outcomes of restorative processes are recognized and implemented within the legal framework. This collaboration enhances the effectiveness and legitimacy of restorative justice.

Conclusion

The success of restorative justice relies on the active participation and collaboration of multiple stakeholders. Victims, offenders, facilitators, community members, and justice professionals each play a crucial role in creating a holistic and inclusive approach to resolving conflict and harm. By working together, these stakeholders contribute to a justice system that prioritizes healing, accountability, and reconciliation, ultimately promoting long-term peace and social cohesion. As we continue to explore and expand restorative justice practices, the involvement and commitment of these key stakeholders will remain essential to achieving meaningful and transformative outcomes.

CHAPTER 02

THE PROCESS OF VICTIM-OFFENDER MEDIATION

Preparation and Assessment

Victim-offender mediation is a structured process that requires careful preparation and assessment to ensure its effectiveness. This phase is crucial as it sets the foundation for a constructive and meaningful dialogue between the victim and the offender. Preparation and assessment involve screening for suitability, obtaining informed consent, and preparing participants for the mediation process. Facilitators play a key role in this stage, ensuring that both victims and offenders are willing and ready to engage constructively. This chapter delves into the essential steps involved in the preparation and assessment phase of victim-offender mediation.

Screening for Suitability

The first step in the preparation and assessment process is screening to determine whether a case is suitable for victim-offender mediation. Not all cases are appropriate for mediation, and it is important to assess the specifics of each situation carefully.

Factors to Consider in Screening:

1. Nature of the Offense: Certain types of offenses, such as violent crimes or cases involving significant power imbalances, may require careful consideration to determine if mediation is appropriate. The safety and well-being of the victim are paramount.

2. Willingness to Participate: Both the victim and the offender must be willing to participate voluntarily. Coercion or pressure to engage in mediation can undermine the process and its outcomes.

3. Readiness for Dialogue: Participants must be emotionally and mentally prepared for the mediation process. This includes a willingness to engage in open dialogue and to consider the perspectives of the other party.

4. Potential for Resolution: The likelihood of reaching a constructive resolution should be considered. This involves

assessing whether the offender is willing to take responsibility and whether the victim is open to dialogue and potential restitution.

Screening Process:

- Initial Assessment: Facilitators conduct an initial assessment through interviews or questionnaires to gather information about the offense, the participant's willingness to engage, and their readiness for mediation.

- Risk Assessment: A risk assessment is conducted to ensure the safety of all participants. This includes evaluating any potential risks associated with bringing the victim and offender together and determining how to mitigate these risks.

- Consultation with Stakeholders: Facilitators may consult with other stakeholders, such as law enforcement, social workers, or legal professionals, to gather additional insights and to ensure a comprehensive understanding of the case.

Obtaining Informed Consent

Informed consent is a critical component of the preparation and assessment phase. It ensures that participants fully understand the mediation process, its goals, and their roles and responsibilities. Obtaining informed consent involves providing clear and comprehensive information to both victims and offenders.

Elements of Informed Consent:

1. Explanation of the Process: Participants must receive a detailed explanation of the mediation process, including its structure, stages, and expected outcomes. This helps set realistic expectations and ensures transparency.

2. Voluntary Participation: It is essential to emphasize that participation in mediation is voluntary. Participants should understand that they have the right to withdraw from the process at any time without facing negative consequences.

3. Confidentiality: The confidentiality of the mediation process must be explained. Participants should be informed that the discussions and agreements reached during mediation will not be disclosed without their consent.

4. Roles and Responsibilities: Participants need to understand their roles and responsibilities within the mediation process. This includes the importance of honest communication, mutual respect, and a commitment to the agreed-upon outcomes.

Process of Obtaining Informed Consent:

- Information Sessions: Facilitators conduct information sessions with both victims and offenders, either individually or together, to explain the mediation process and address any questions or concerns.

- Written Consent Forms: Participants are provided with written consent forms that outline the key elements of the mediation process. These forms must be read, understood, and signed by both parties to confirm their informed consent.

- Ongoing Communication: Facilitators maintain ongoing communication with participants to ensure that they continue to understand and agree to the process as it progresses. Any changes or new developments are communicated promptly.

Preparing Participants for Mediation

Effective preparation of participants is crucial for the success of the mediation process. This involves helping both victims and offenders understand what to expect, addressing their concerns, and building their readiness for constructive engagement.

Preparation Steps:

1. Pre-Mediation Meetings: Facilitators conduct pre-mediation meetings with both victims and offenders to discuss the mediation process in detail. These meetings provide an opportunity to build rapport, address any anxieties, and clarify expectations.

2. Emotional Support: Participants may experience a range of emotions, including anxiety, anger, or fear. Facilitators provide emotional support and guidance, helping participants manage their emotions and prepare for the dialogue.

3. Skill Building: Facilitators may engage participants in skill-building exercises to enhance their communication and conflict resolution skills. This can include active listening, expressing emotions constructively, and developing empathy.

4. Setting Goals: Participants are encouraged to set personal goals for the mediation process. This helps them focus on the desired outcomes and understand their own needs and expectations.

Pre-Mediation Meetings:

- For Victims: Pre-mediation meetings with victims focus on understanding their experiences, needs, and concerns. Facilitators provide a safe space for victims to express their emotions and prepare them for the dialogue with the offender.

- For Offenders: Pre-mediation meetings with offenders emphasize the importance of taking responsibility and understanding the impact of their actions. Facilitators guide offenders in reflecting on their behavior and preparing for a meaningful dialogue with the victim.

Building Readiness:

- Addressing Concerns: Facilitators address any concerns or fears that participants may have about the mediation process. This includes providing reassurance, answering questions, and ensuring that participants feel supported.

- Setting Ground Rules: Establishing clear ground rules for the mediation process is essential. These rules ensure that the dialogue remains respectful, constructive, and focused on healing and resolution.

- Creating a Safe Environment: Facilitators work to create a safe and supportive environment for the mediation process. This involves considering the physical setting, timing, and any accommodations needed to ensure participants feel comfortable and secure.

Conclusion

The preparation and assessment phase is a critical component of the victim-offender mediation process. By conducting thorough screening, obtaining informed consent, and preparing participants for mediation, facilitators lay the groundwork for a successful and constructive dialogue. This phase ensures that both victims and offenders are willing, ready, and supported as they engage in the mediation process. As we continue to explore and implement restorative justice practices, the importance of careful preparation and assessment cannot be overstated. These steps are essential to achieving meaningful and transformative outcomes that promote healing, accountability, and reconciliation.

Facilitating the Mediation Session

The mediation session is the heart of the victim-offender mediation process, where the principles of restorative justice are put into practice. This structured yet flexible process provides an opportunity for victims and offenders to engage in meaningful dialogue, guided by facilitators who ensure a respectful and empathetic exchange. The ultimate goal is to reach a shared understanding of the harm caused and to develop a plan for restitution and reparation. This chapter explores the key elements of facilitating a successful mediation session, from setting the stage to ensuring follow-up.

Setting the Stage

Creating a conducive environment for the mediation session is crucial. This involves careful planning and attention to detail to ensure that participants feel safe, respected, and ready to engage.

Choosing the Right Venue:

1. Neutral Location: Select a neutral, comfortable, and private location where both parties feel at ease. The setting should be free from distractions and interruptions to facilitate open dialogue.

2. Accessibility: Ensure the venue is accessible to all participants, considering factors such as transportation, physical accessibility, and any special needs.

Timing and Logistics:

1. Scheduling: Choose a time that works for all parties, allowing sufficient time for the session without rushing. It is important to allocate enough time for thorough discussion and resolution.

2. Preparation: Ensure all necessary materials, such as seating arrangements, refreshments, and mediation tools (e.g., flip charts, and pens), are in place before the session begins.

Creating a Safe and Respectful Atmosphere:

1. Ground Rules: Establish clear ground rules at the outset to ensure a respectful and productive dialogue. Common ground rules include speaking one at a time, listening without interruption, and maintaining confidentiality.

2. Confidentiality: Emphasize the importance of confidentiality, reassuring participants that what is discussed in the session will remain private unless they agree otherwise.

Guiding the Conversation

The facilitator's role is to guide the conversation, ensuring that it remains respectful, focused, and empathetic. Effective facilitation requires a balance of structure and flexibility, allowing the dialogue to flow naturally while keeping it on track.

Opening the Session:

1. Introductions: Begin with introductions, allowing participants to share a bit about themselves. This helps build rapport and sets a positive tone for the session.

2. Purpose and Objectives: Clearly state the purpose of the mediation and the objectives of the session. Emphasize the goal of reaching a shared understanding and developing a plan for restitution.

Encouraging Open Dialogue:

1. Active Listening: Demonstrate active listening by paying close attention to what each participant says, nodding, and providing verbal affirmations. Reflect on key points to show understanding.

2. Empathy and Validation: Show empathy and validation for participants' feelings and experiences. Acknowledge their emotions and the impact of the harm caused.

3. Open-Ended Questions: Use open-ended questions to encourage deeper exploration and discussion. Questions like "Can you tell us more about how this has affected you?" or "What do you think needs to happen to make things right?" can facilitate meaningful dialogue.

Managing Emotions and Conflict:

1. De-escalation Techniques: Be prepared to use de-escalation techniques if emotions run high. This can include taking breaks, using calming language, and redirecting the conversation to focus on solutions.

2. Maintaining Neutrality: Maintain neutrality and avoid taking sides. Ensure that both parties feel heard and respected and that their perspectives are valued.

Structuring the Dialogue:

1. Storytelling: Encourage both victims and offenders to share their stories. This can help build mutual understanding and empathy. Allow each participant to speak without interruption.

2. Exploring Impact: Guide the conversation to explore the impact of the crime on the victim, the offender, and the community. This helps participants understand the broader context and consequences of the offense.

3. Identifying Needs: Facilitate a discussion about the needs of both victims and offenders. What do they need to

move forward? What would help repair the harm and restore balance?

Developing a Plan for Restitution and Reparation

Once a shared understanding of the harm has been reached, the focus shifts to developing a plan for restitution and reparation. This plan should be collaborative, realistic, and tailored to the specific needs and circumstances of the participants.

Collaborative Problem-Solving:

1. Brainstorming Solutions: Encourage participants to brainstorm potential solutions and ways to make amends. Allow for creative and diverse ideas, and ensure that all suggestions are considered.

2. Negotiation and Compromise: Facilitate negotiation and compromise to reach mutually agreeable solutions. Help participants find common ground and work through differences.

Formulating the Agreement:

1. Specific Actions: Ensure that the agreement includes specific actions that the offender will take to make amends. This could include financial compensation, community service, apologies, or other forms of restitution.

2. Realistic and Achievable: The plan should be realistic and achievable, considering the capacities and

resources of the offender. Overly ambitious plans may set participants up for failure and disappointment.

3. Timelines and Follow-Up: Establish clear timelines for completing the agreed-upon actions. Include provisions for follow-up to ensure that commitments are met and to address any issues that arise.

Documenting the Agreement:

1. Written Agreement: Document the agreement in writing, outlining the specific actions, timelines, and responsibilities. Ensure that both parties understand and agree to the terms.

2. Signatures: Obtain signatures from both the victim and the offender, as well as the facilitator, to formalize the agreement. This adds a sense of commitment and accountability.

Closing the Session

Closing the mediation session on a positive note is important for reinforcing the progress made and the commitments agreed upon. It also provides an opportunity to address any final questions or concerns.

Reviewing the Agreement:

1. Summary: Review the agreement with all participants, summarizing the key points and actions to be

taken. Ensure that everyone is clear on their roles and responsibilities.

2. Next Steps: Outline the next steps, including any follow-up meetings or check-ins to monitor progress. Provide contact information for participants to reach out if they have questions or need support.

Expressing Gratitude:

1. Acknowledgment: Acknowledge the courage and willingness of both victims and offenders to participate in the mediation process. Thank them for their openness and commitment to resolution.

2. Support and Resources: Offer additional support and resources, such as counseling or community services, to help participants continue their healing and reintegration journey.

Final Reflections:

1. Reflection Time: Allow a few moments for participants to reflect on the session and share any final thoughts or feelings. This can provide closure and reinforce the positive outcomes of the mediation.

2. Positive Reinforcement: Reinforce the positive aspects of the session, highlighting the progress made and the potential for healing and reconciliation.

Ensuring Follow-Up

Follow-up is a crucial aspect of the mediation process, ensuring that the agreements reached are implemented and that participants continue to receive support.

Monitoring Progress:

1. Check-Ins: Schedule regular check-ins with both the victim and the offender to monitor progress on the agreed-upon actions. These check-ins can be in-person meetings, phone calls, or written updates.

2. Addressing Issues: Be prepared to address any issues or challenges that arise during the implementation of the agreement. Offer additional mediation sessions if needed to resolve any conflicts or misunderstandings.

Providing Ongoing Support:

1. Counseling and Services: Offer referrals to counseling, support groups, or other services that can help participants continue their healing and reintegration process.

2. Community Resources: Connect participants with community resources that can provide ongoing support and assistance. This can include legal aid, financial assistance, or social services.

Evaluating Outcomes:

1. Feedback and Evaluation: Collect feedback from participants on their experience with the mediation process.

This can provide valuable insights for improving future mediation sessions.

2. Measuring Impact: Evaluate the impact of the mediation on both the victim and the offender, as well as on the community. Consider factors such as emotional healing, reduced recidivism, and enhanced social cohesion.

Conclusion

Facilitating the mediation session is a delicate and crucial part of the victim-offender mediation process. By setting the stage, guiding the conversation, developing a plan for restitution, closing the session positively, and ensuring follow-up, facilitators can help create a constructive and transformative experience for all participants. The success of the mediation session relies on the skills, empathy, and dedication of the facilitators, as well as the willingness and commitment of the victims and offenders. As we continue to explore and implement restorative justice practices, the role of effective facilitation in achieving meaningful outcomes cannot be overstated.

Follow-Up and Implementation of Agreements

Victim-offender mediation is not complete once the mediation session concludes. The true measure of its success lies in the effective implementation of the agreements reached and the ongoing support provided to both victims and offenders. Follow-up is a critical component of the restorative justice process, ensuring that the commitments made during mediation are honored and that all parties continue to receive the necessary support. This chapter explores the steps and strategies involved in follow-up and implementation, emphasizing the importance of monitoring progress, providing additional resources, and facilitating further dialogue as needed.

Monitoring Progress

Effective follow-up begins with regular monitoring of the progress made towards fulfilling the agreements. This ensures that both parties remain accountable and that any challenges or obstacles are promptly addressed.

Scheduling Check-Ins:

1. Regular Check-Ins: Schedule regular check-ins with both the victim and the offender to discuss progress and address any concerns. These can be in-person meetings, phone calls, or virtual sessions, depending on what is most convenient for the participants.

2. Frequency: The frequency of check-ins may vary based on the complexity of the agreement and the needs of the participants. Initially, more frequent check-ins may be necessary, with the possibility of reducing frequency as progress is made.

Tracking Progress:

1. Progress Reports: Encourage participants to provide progress reports on their actions. Offenders can report on the steps they have taken to fulfill their commitments, while victims can share their observations and any ongoing needs.

2. Documentation: Keep detailed records of all follow-up interactions, including the dates of check-ins, the progress reported, and any issues or concerns raised. This documentation helps in tracking the implementation and identifying any patterns or recurring issues.

Addressing Challenges:

1. Identifying Barriers: Identify any barriers or obstacles that may hinder the implementation of the agreement. This could include logistical challenges, lack of resources, or emotional and psychological factors.

2. Problem-Solving: Work collaboratively with participants to develop strategies for overcoming these barriers. This may involve adjusting the agreement, providing additional support, or finding alternative solutions.

Providing Additional Resources

Supporting the implementation of mediation agreements often requires providing participants with additional resources and assistance. This support can help ensure that the agreements are realistic and achievable.

Counseling and Support Services:

1. Access to Counseling: Offer access to counseling services for both victims and offenders. Counseling can provide emotional support, help address trauma, and facilitate personal growth and healing.

2. Support Groups: Connect participants with support groups where they can share their experiences and receive encouragement from others who have gone through similar processes.

Educational and Vocational Programs:

1. Education and Training: Provide information on educational and vocational programs that can help offenders gain new skills and improve their chances of successful reintegration into society.

2. Job Placement Assistance: Offer job placement assistance and resources to help offenders find employment, which can be a crucial factor in reducing recidivism and promoting rehabilitation.

Financial and Legal Assistance:

1. Financial Support: If the agreement involves financial restitution, provide guidance on financial

management and, if necessary, access to financial assistance programs.

2. Legal Aid: Offer legal aid services to help participants navigate any legal issues related to the agreement or their broader circumstances.

Community Resources:

1. Community Programs: Connect participants with community programs and services that can provide ongoing support. This could include housing assistance, substance abuse programs, or social services.

2. Mentorship Programs: Encourage participation in mentorship programs where offenders can receive guidance and support from positive role models within the community.

Facilitating Further Dialogue

In some cases, additional dialogue sessions may be necessary to address ongoing issues, renegotiate agreements, or provide further support. Facilitators play a key role in organizing and guiding these sessions.

Follow-Up Mediation Sessions:

1. Renegotiating Agreements: If the original agreement is not working or needs adjustment, schedule follow-up mediation sessions to renegotiate the terms. This ensures that the agreement remains relevant and achievable.

2. Addressing New Issues: Use follow-up sessions to address any new issues that may have arisen since the initial mediation. This can help prevent conflicts from escalating and ensure that both parties continue to feel supported.

Continuous Communication:

1. Open Lines of Communication: Maintain open lines of communication with both victims and offenders, encouraging them to reach out if they encounter any difficulties or have concerns about the implementation process.

2. Facilitator Availability: Ensure that facilitators are available to provide guidance and support as needed. This ongoing availability can help participants feel more secure and confident in fulfilling their commitments.

Building Long-Term Relationships:

1. Strengthening Relationships: Foster the development of long-term relationships between participants and support networks, such as community members, mentors, or support groups. These relationships can provide ongoing encouragement and assistance.

2. Community Engagement: Encourage participants to engage with their communities through volunteer work, community service, or participation in local events. This

engagement can help build a sense of belonging and reinforce positive behavior.

Evaluating Outcomes

Evaluation is an essential component of the follow-up process, providing insights into the effectiveness of the mediation and the impact of the agreements on participants and the community.

Collecting Feedback:

1. Participant Surveys: Conduct surveys or interviews with participants to gather feedback on their experience with the mediation process and the follow-up support provided. This feedback can highlight areas of success and identify opportunities for improvement.

2. Stakeholder Input: Seek input from other stakeholders involved in the mediation, such as facilitators, support service providers, and community members. Their perspectives can provide a more comprehensive understanding of the outcomes.

Measuring Impact:

1. Quantitative Metrics: Use quantitative metrics to measure the impact of the mediation, such as the completion rate of agreed-upon actions, recidivism rates, and levels of victim satisfaction.

2. Qualitative Insights: Gather qualitative insights through participant narratives and case studies. These stories can illustrate the personal and relational transformations that occur as a result of the mediation process.

Continuous Improvement:

1. Identifying Best Practices: Use the evaluation data to identify best practices and effective strategies that can be applied to future mediations. This continuous learning process helps improve the overall quality and effectiveness of restorative justice programs.

2. Adapting Programs: Be open to adapting and refining mediation programs based on the evaluation findings. This flexibility ensures that the programs remain responsive to the needs of participants and the community.

Conclusion

The follow-up and implementation phase is a vital part of the victim-offender mediation process, ensuring that the agreements reached during mediation are effectively carried out and that participants continue to receive the support they need. By monitoring progress, providing additional resources, facilitating further dialogue, and evaluating outcomes, facilitators and stakeholders can help create lasting positive change for both victims and offenders. This ongoing commitment to follow-up reinforces the principles of restorative justice, promoting healing, accountability, and reconciliation. As we continue to develop and refine restorative justice practices, the importance of thorough and supportive follow-up cannot be overstated. It is through these efforts that the true potential of restorative justice can be realized, fostering stronger, more resilient communities.

CHAPTER 03

BENEFITS OF VICTIM-OFFENDER MEDIATION

For Victims: Healing and Empowerment

Victim-offender mediation offers profound benefits for victims, providing a path toward healing and empowerment that is often lacking in traditional justice systems. This chapter explores how the mediation process helps victims by giving them a voice, answering their questions, offering closure, and allowing them to actively participate in the justice process. These elements collectively contribute to the emotional and psychological healing of victims and restore a sense of control and agency.

Providing a Voice to Victims

One of the primary benefits of victim-offender mediation is that it provides victims with a platform to voice their experiences and emotions. In traditional justice systems, victims often feel marginalized and unheard, with their needs and perspectives overshadowed by legal procedures focused on the offender.

Expression of Emotions:

1. Sharing Experiences: Mediation allows victims to share their personal experiences of the crime, including the emotional, psychological, and physical impact. This expression is crucial for validation and acknowledgment of their suffering.

2. Releasing Emotions: The process provides a safe space for victims to release pent-up emotions, such as anger, fear, and sadness, which can be therapeutic and facilitate emotional healing.

Empowerment Through Storytelling:

1. Narrative Control: By telling their story in their own words, victims regain narrative control. This can counter feelings of helplessness and victimization, empowering them to reclaim their identity and strength.

2. Recognition and Validation: Hearing their story validated by the offender and others involved in the mediation process reinforces the victim's sense of worth and dignity, contributing to their healing journey.

Answering Questions and Seeking Understanding

Victims often have unanswered questions about the crime and its context, which can hinder their ability to move forward. Victim-offender mediation offers an opportunity to seek understanding and clarity directly from the offender.

Addressing Unanswered Questions:

1. Why and How: Victims can ask offenders why they committed the crime and how it came about. Understanding the motives and circumstances can provide closure and reduce feelings of confusion and anger.

2. Impact of Actions: Offenders can explain their actions and acknowledge their impact, helping victims understand the broader context and humanizing the offender. This understanding can be a crucial step toward forgiveness and healing.

Fostering Empathy and Reconciliation:

1. Building Empathy: The dialogue fosters empathy by allowing both parties to see each other as individuals with emotions and experiences. This mutual understanding can reduce hostility and promote reconciliation.

2. Creating Connection: Victims may find that hearing the offender's story creates a sense of connection, breaking down barriers and facilitating a more profound sense of closure and healing.

Achieving Closure and Moving Forward

Closure is an essential aspect of healing for victims. Victim-offender mediation helps achieve closure by addressing unresolved issues, providing emotional release, and facilitating a sense of finality.

Emotional Release:

1. Confronting the Offender: Facing the offender and expressing the impact of the crime can be a powerful emotional release for victims. It allows them to confront their pain and begin the process of letting go.

2. Receiving Apologies: Hearing a sincere apology from the offender can validate the victim's feelings and experiences, providing a sense of justice and contributing to emotional healing.

Finality and Resolution:

1. Reaching Agreements: Developing mutually agreed-upon plans for restitution and reparation provides a concrete sense of resolution. Knowing that steps are being taken to address the harm can help victims find peace.

2. Moving Beyond the Crime: The mediation process allows victims to move beyond the role of a victim, enabling them to focus on their future and personal growth. This shift in identity is crucial for long-term healing and empowerment.

Active Participation in the Justice Process

Victim-offender mediation empowers victims by involving them directly in the justice process. Unlike traditional systems where victims are passive observers, mediation makes them active participants.

Agency and Control:

1. Active Involvement: Victims actively participate in discussions and decision-making, giving them a sense of agency and control over the outcomes. This involvement contrasts sharply with the often passive role they play in conventional justice systems.

2. Shaping Outcomes: By contributing to the development of restitution plans, victims can ensure that their needs and interests are addressed. This direct input into the justice process is empowering and validating.

Empowerment and Healing:

1. Restoring Balance: Active participation helps restore a sense of balance and justice for victims. They see tangible actions being taken to address the harm, which can affirm their faith in the justice system and society.

2. Building Confidence: Engaging in the mediation process can build victims' confidence and self-esteem. Successfully navigating the process and achieving a positive outcome reinforces their sense of strength and resilience.

Psychological and Emotional Benefits

The psychological and emotional benefits of victim-offender mediation are profound. The process addresses the emotional wounds inflicted by the crime and promotes holistic healing.

Psychological Healing:

1. Reducing Anxiety and Fear: Confronting the offender in a controlled and supportive environment can reduce anxiety and fear. Victims often find that the offender is less intimidating when they are able to interact directly and humanize them.

2. Alleviating Anger and Resentment: Expressing their feelings and receiving acknowledgment from the offender can help alleviate feelings of anger and resentment, which are common emotional responses to victimization.

Emotional Resilience:

1. Developing Coping Mechanisms: The mediation process helps victims develop coping mechanisms to deal with their trauma. This resilience is crucial for overcoming the long-term effects of crime.

2. Fostering Hope and Optimism: Seeing positive changes in the offender and witnessing the commitment to making amends can foster hope and optimism in victims. It reassures them that people can change and that justice can be restorative.

Conclusion

Victim-offender mediation provides significant benefits for victims, offering a path toward healing and empowerment that is often absent in traditional justice systems. By giving victims a voice, answering their questions, providing closure, and involving them actively in the justice process, mediation helps restore their sense of control and dignity. The psychological and emotional benefits of this approach are profound, contributing to the overall healing and well-being of victims. As we continue to expand and refine restorative justice practices, the empowerment and healing of victims will remain a central focus, ensuring that justice is not only served but also restorative and transformative.

For Offenders: Accountability and Rehabilitation

Victim-offender mediation offers significant benefits for offenders by promoting accountability and facilitating rehabilitation. This chapter explores how the mediation process helps offenders take responsibility for their actions, understand the impact on victims, and engage in meaningful efforts to make amends. Through these experiences, offenders can develop genuine remorse, commit to positive changes, and reduce the likelihood of reoffending.

Promoting Accountability

One of the primary benefits of victim-offender mediation for offenders is the promotion of accountability. Traditional justice systems often focus on punishment, which may not encourage offenders to take full responsibility for their actions. In contrast, restorative justice emphasizes accountability as a pathway to personal growth and rehabilitation.

Understanding the Impact:

1. Hearing Victims' Stories: During the mediation session, offenders listen to the victims' accounts of how the crime has affected their lives. This direct exposure to the victims' experiences can be eye-opening and transformative, helping offenders understand the real impact of their actions.

2. Acknowledging Harm: Offenders are encouraged to acknowledge the harm they have caused. This acknowledgment is a crucial step in taking responsibility and moving beyond denial or minimization of their actions.

Expressing Remorse:

1. Sincere Apologies: The mediation process provides offenders with an opportunity to express genuine remorse and apologize directly to the victims. This can be a powerful and healing experience for both parties.

2. Empathy Development: By engaging with the victims' emotions and experiences, offenders can develop

empathy, which is essential for genuine remorse and accountability.

Engaging in Dialogue:

1. Open Communication: The structured dialogue in mediation allows offenders to communicate openly about the circumstances that led to their actions. This can help them articulate their thoughts and feelings, leading to a deeper understanding of their behavior.

2. Mutual Understanding: Through dialogue, offenders and victims can achieve mutual understanding, which can break down barriers and reduce feelings of animosity. This mutual understanding fosters a more constructive approach to accountability.

Facilitating Rehabilitation

Rehabilitation is a key goal of restorative justice, and victim-offender mediation plays a crucial role in facilitating this process. By promoting accountability and providing opportunities for personal growth, mediation helps offenders embark on a path toward rehabilitation.

Commitment to Change:

1. Personal Reflection: The mediation process encourages offenders to reflect on their behavior and its consequences. This reflection can lead to a commitment to change and to making better choices in the future.

2. Goal Setting: Offenders can set personal goals for rehabilitation, such as completing education or vocational training, addressing substance abuse issues, or improving relationships with family and community members.

Developing Reparation Plans:

1. Concrete Actions: Offenders work with victims to develop concrete plans for restitution and reparation. These plans often include actions that offenders can take to make amends, such as financial compensation, community service, or personal acts of reparation.

2. Sense of Accomplishment: Successfully completing the agreed-upon actions provides offenders with a sense of accomplishment and reinforces their commitment to positive change.

Support and Resources:

1. Access to Services: Facilitators and support networks can connect offenders with services and resources that support their rehabilitation. This may include counseling, educational programs, job placement services, and substance abuse treatment.

2. Ongoing Monitoring: Regular follow-up and monitoring help ensure that offenders stay on track with their rehabilitation goals and receive the necessary support to overcome challenges.

Reducing Recidivism

One of the most significant benefits of victim-offender mediation is its potential to reduce recidivism. Offenders who engage in the mediation process are often less likely to re-offend, as the experience fosters personal growth, accountability, and a commitment to positive behavior.

Understanding Consequences:

1. Realizing Impact: Offenders gain a deeper understanding of the consequences of their actions, not just legally but emotionally and socially. This awareness can deter future criminal behavior by making offenders more mindful of the impact of their actions.

2. Developing Empathy: Empathy developed through the mediation process can reduce the likelihood of reoffending. Offenders who understand and care about the harm they have caused are less likely to repeat their behavior.

Building Positive Relationships:

1. Restoring Relationships: The mediation process can help restore relationships between offenders and their families, communities, and even victims. Positive relationships provide support and motivation for offenders to maintain good behavior.

2. Community Reintegration: Successful mediation and the resulting positive changes in behavior can facilitate

the reintegration of offenders into their communities. Feeling accepted and supported reduces the chances of returning to criminal activity.

Encouraging Pro-Social Behavior:

1. Positive Role Models: Mediation can connect offenders with positive role models and mentors who guide and support their rehabilitation journey. These influences encourage pro-social behavior and provide a network of support.

2. Engagement in Community: Community service and other reparative actions promote engagement in positive community activities. Offenders who feel valued and connected to their community are less likely to engage in criminal behavior.

Emotional and Psychological Benefits

The emotional and psychological benefits of victim-offender mediation for offenders are profound. The process addresses the internal factors that contribute to criminal behavior and supports the emotional well-being of offenders.

Emotional Healing:

1. Addressing Guilt and Shame: The mediation process helps offenders address feelings of guilt and shame associated with their actions. By taking responsibility and making amends, offenders can begin to heal emotionally.

2. Developing Self-Respect: Successfully participating in mediation and fulfilling commitments can help offenders develop self-respect and a sense of pride in their ability to change.

Building Resilience:

1. Coping Skills: Mediation helps offenders develop coping skills to manage stress, anger, and other emotions that may contribute to criminal behavior. These skills are essential for maintaining positive behavior.

2. Positive Identity: Engaging in the mediation process and committing to positive change allows offenders to develop a new, positive identity. This shift in self-perception is crucial for long-term rehabilitation and personal growth.

Conclusion

Victim-offender mediation offers significant benefits for offenders, promoting accountability, facilitating rehabilitation, and reducing the likelihood of reoffending. By taking responsibility for their actions, understanding the impact on victims, and engaging in meaningful efforts to make amends, offenders can develop genuine remorse and commit to positive changes. The mediation process supports emotional and psychological healing, helping offenders build resilience and a positive identity. As we continue to expand and refine restorative justice practices, the focus on accountability and rehabilitation for offenders will remain central to achieving meaningful and transformative outcomes, fostering safer and more supportive communities.

For Communities: Strengthening Social Fabric

Restorative justice not only benefits victims and offenders but also has a profound impact on the broader community. By promoting values of empathy, respect, and mutual support, restorative justice helps strengthen the social fabric of communities. It fosters a culture of accountability and reconciliation, reducing social isolation and the stigma associated with crime. This chapter explores how restorative justice processes, particularly victim-offender mediation, contribute to community cohesion, resilience, and overall well-being.

Promoting Empathy and Understanding

One of the core principles of restorative justice is fostering empathy and understanding among all parties involved in the justice process. By encouraging open dialogue and shared experiences, restorative justice helps build a more compassionate and connected community.

Building Bridges Between Individuals:

1. Humanizing the Offender: Through mediation, community members get to see offenders as individuals with complex backgrounds and experiences. This humanization

reduces stereotypes and prejudices, fostering a more inclusive community.

2. Victim Stories: Hearing victims' stories can elicit empathy and support from community members, who may then become more proactive in supporting victims and preventing crime.

Enhancing Social Cohesion:

1. Shared Responsibility: Restorative justice emphasizes that crime affects the entire community and that everyone has a role in addressing and preventing it. This shared responsibility strengthens community bonds and collective action.

2. Mutual Support: Communities that practice restorative justice develop a culture of mutual support, where members look out for one another and work together to resolve conflicts and support those affected by crime.

Fostering a Culture of Accountability

Restorative justice promotes a culture of accountability, where individuals are encouraged to take responsibility for their actions and make amends. This cultural shift can lead to more responsible and ethical behavior within the community.

Encouraging Responsible Behavior:

1. Community Standards: Restorative justice helps establish and reinforce community standards of behavior. When offenders take responsibility and make amends, it sets a positive example for others, promoting a culture of accountability.

2. Peer Influence: Offenders who go through the restorative justice process can influence their peers by demonstrating the importance of taking responsibility for their actions and the benefits of making amends.

Reducing Recidivism:

1. Supportive Environment: A community that embraces restorative justice provides a supportive environment for offenders to reintegrate and rebuild their lives. This support reduces the likelihood of reoffending, as individuals feel valued and connected to their community.

2. Preventive Measures: Restorative justice encourages preventive measures, such as community programs and education, that address the root causes of crime and promote pro-social behavior.

Enhancing Community Resilience

Restorative justice contributes to building resilient communities that can effectively respond to and recover from crime and conflict. By focusing on healing and restoration, restorative justice helps communities become more adaptable and cohesive.

Building Trust and Cooperation:

1. Collaborative Problem-Solving: Restorative justice involves collaborative problem-solving, where community members work together to address the harm caused by crime and find solutions. This cooperation builds trust and strengthens social ties.

2. Inclusive Decision-Making: The inclusive nature of restorative justice ensures that all voices are heard and considered in the decision-making process. This inclusivity fosters a sense of belonging and collective ownership of community outcomes.

Supporting Vulnerable Members:

1. Addressing Needs: Restorative justice processes prioritize the needs of victims and offenders, ensuring that vulnerable community members receive the support and resources they need to heal and reintegrate.

2. Empowerment: By involving community members in the justice process, restorative justice empowers individuals to take an active role in shaping their community and supporting one another.

Reducing Social Isolation and Stigma

Crime and conflict can lead to social isolation and stigma for both victims and offenders. Restorative justice helps reduce these negative impacts by promoting understanding, acceptance, and reintegration.

Supporting Victims:

1. Community Involvement: When the community actively supports victims through restorative justice processes, it reduces the isolation and stigma that victims may feel. This support helps victims feel valued and connected to their community.

2. Public Acknowledgment: Public acknowledgment of the harm caused to victims and the community's role in their healing process can help reduce stigma and promote a more compassionate response to victimization.

Reintegrating Offenders:

1. Restorative Practices: Restorative justice practices focus on the reintegration of offenders, helping them rebuild their lives and relationships within the community. This reintegration reduces the stigma associated with criminal behavior.

2. Community Acceptance: When offenders successfully complete restitution and demonstrate a commitment to change, the community is more likely to

accept and support their reintegration, reducing social isolation.

Strengthening Community Institutions

Restorative justice can also strengthen community institutions by promoting more effective and inclusive approaches to conflict resolution and justice.

Educational Institutions:

1. Restorative Practices in Schools: Implementing restorative practices in schools can reduce disciplinary issues, improve student behavior, and create a more positive school environment. This approach helps students learn accountability, empathy, and conflict-resolution skills.

2. Peer Mediation Programs: Peer mediation programs empower students to resolve conflicts among themselves, promoting a culture of peace and mutual respect within the school community.

Workplaces and Organizations:

1. Conflict Resolution: Restorative justice can be applied in workplaces and organizations to address conflicts and grievances. This approach fosters a more collaborative and respectful work environment.

2. Employee Support: By addressing the needs of employees affected by conflict or harm, restorative justice promotes employee well-being and productivity.

Law Enforcement and Justice Systems:

1. Community Policing: Restorative justice principles can enhance community policing efforts by building trust and cooperation between law enforcement and community members. This partnership improves public safety and reduces crime.

2. Restorative Programs: Incorporating restorative programs within the justice system can provide alternative pathways for addressing crime, reducing the burden on traditional courts, and promoting more positive outcomes for all parties involved.

Fostering a Restorative Culture

A restorative culture is one where the principles and practices of restorative justice are deeply embedded in the community's way of life. This culture promotes ongoing healing, reconciliation, and mutual support.

Community Norms:

1. Restorative Values: By consistently applying restorative justice principles, communities can establish norms of empathy, respect, and accountability. These values

guide behavior and interactions, creating a more harmonious and supportive environment.

2. Ongoing Education: Providing ongoing education and training on restorative justice helps community members understand and embrace its principles. This education can include workshops, seminars, and community discussions.

Celebrating Successes:

1. Public Recognition: Publicly recognizing the successes of restorative justice initiatives reinforces the positive impact of these practices and encourages continued participation and support.

2. Sharing Stories: Sharing stories of healing and reconciliation within the community can inspire others to engage in restorative practices and contribute to the overall culture of support and empathy.

Conclusion

Restorative justice has far-reaching benefits for communities, strengthening the social fabric by promoting values of empathy, respect, and mutual support. By fostering a culture of accountability and reconciliation, restorative justice reduces social isolation and stigma associated with crime. It enhances community resilience, builds trust and cooperation, and supports the reintegration of offenders. As communities continue to embrace and implement restorative justice practices, they become more cohesive, resilient, and compassionate, ultimately creating a safer and more supportive environment for all members.

CHAPTER 04

THE ROLE OF MEDIATORS

Qualifications and Training

Mediators play a critical role in the success of victim-offender mediation and other restorative justice processes. Effective mediators require specialized training and qualifications that equip them with the necessary skills and knowledge to facilitate constructive dialogue and resolution. This chapter explores the essential qualifications and training needed for mediators, emphasizing the importance of restorative justice principles, conflict resolution skills, and an understanding of psychological and emotional dynamics. Additionally, it highlights the significance of ongoing education and certification to maintain high standards of practice.

Core Qualifications for Mediators

Effective mediators possess a combination of academic qualifications, practical skills, and personal attributes that enable them to facilitate restorative justice processes successfully.

Academic Background:

1. Relevant Degrees: While not always mandatory, many effective mediators hold degrees in fields such as psychology, social work, law, criminal justice, or conflict resolution. These academic backgrounds provide a solid foundation in understanding human behavior, legal principles, and conflict dynamics.

2. Restorative Justice Education: Specialized education in restorative justice principles and practices is highly beneficial. This can include courses or certifications from recognized institutions that focus on the theory and application of restorative justice.

Practical Skills:

1. Conflict Resolution: Mediators must be skilled in conflict resolution techniques, including negotiation, mediation, and facilitation. These skills enable them to guide parties through the mediation process and help them reach mutually agreeable solutions.

2. Communication Skills: Strong communication skills are essential for mediators. They must be able to listen actively, articulate thoughts clearly, and facilitate open and respectful dialogue between parties.

3. Emotional Intelligence: Mediators need high levels of emotional intelligence, including empathy, self-awareness, and the ability to manage their own emotions. This allows them to understand and respond to the emotional dynamics of the parties involved.

Personal Attributes:

1. Neutrality: Mediators must maintain neutrality and impartiality throughout the mediation process. This means not taking sides and ensuring that all parties feel heard and respected.

2. Patience and Perseverance: Mediating conflicts, especially those involving deep-seated emotions and complex issues, requires patience and perseverance. Mediators must be able to remain calm and composed, even in challenging situations.

3. Cultural Sensitivity: An understanding of and respect for cultural differences is crucial. Mediators must be culturally sensitive and adaptable to the diverse backgrounds and experiences of the participants.

Essential Training for Mediators

Comprehensive training is crucial for developing the skills and knowledge needed to be an effective mediator. This training typically involves a combination of theoretical education, practical exercises, and supervised practice.

Theoretical Education:

1. Restorative Justice Principles: Mediators must have a thorough understanding of restorative justice principles, including the focus on repairing harm, involving all stakeholders, and fostering accountability and reconciliation.

2. Conflict Resolution Theory: Training should cover key conflict resolution theories and models, providing mediators with a framework for understanding and addressing conflicts.

3. Legal and Ethical Considerations: Mediators need to be aware of the legal and ethical considerations involved in restorative justice processes. This includes confidentiality, informed consent, and the legal implications of mediation agreements.

Practical Exercises:

1. Role-Playing Scenarios: Role-playing exercises are an effective way to practice mediation skills in a controlled environment. Trainees can take on the roles of victims, offenders, and mediators to experience different perspectives and refine their techniques.

2. Case Studies: Analyzing case studies of real-life mediation processes helps trainees understand the complexities and challenges they may encounter. This analysis can provide insights into effective strategies and common pitfalls.

3. Simulated Mediations: Simulated mediations allow trainees to practice their skills in a realistic setting. These simulations should be supervised by experienced mediators who can provide feedback and guidance.

Supervised Practice:

1. Mentorship Programs: Participating in mentorship programs allows novice mediators to learn from experienced practitioners. Mentors can provide valuable advice, support, and feedback based on their own experiences.

2. Apprenticeships: Apprenticeships offer hands-on experience under the supervision of a seasoned mediator. Trainees can observe and assist in actual mediation sessions, gradually taking on more responsibility as they gain confidence and competence.

3. Peer Review: Peer review sessions provide an opportunity for mediators to share their experiences, discuss challenges, and receive constructive feedback from their peers. This collaborative learning environment fosters continuous improvement.

Ongoing Education and Certification

To maintain high standards of practice, mediators must engage in ongoing education and seek certification from recognized professional organizations.

Continuing Education:

1. Workshops and Seminars: Attending workshops and seminars on restorative justice, conflict resolution, and related topics helps mediators stay current with the latest research, trends, and best practices.

2. Advanced Training Courses: Enrolling in advanced training courses allows mediators to deepen their knowledge and refine their skills in specific areas, such as trauma-informed mediation or cross-cultural conflict resolution.

3. Professional Development: Participating in professional development programs, such as conferences and webinars, provides opportunities for networking, learning, and sharing experiences with other practitioners.

Certification:

1. Recognized Organizations: Seeking certification from recognized professional organizations, such as the Association for Conflict Resolution (ACR) or the International Institute for Restorative Practices (IIRP), demonstrates a mediator's commitment to professionalism and high standards.

2.	Certification Requirements: Certification requirements typically include a combination of education, training, supervised practice, and continuing education. Mediators must meet these requirements and adhere to the organization's code of ethics and standards of practice.

3. Renewal and Recertification: Certification is often valid for a specific period, after which mediators must renew their certification by demonstrating continued competency and engagement in professional development.

Conclusion

The qualifications and training of mediators are critical to the success of victim-offender mediation and other restorative justice processes. Effective mediators possess a combination of academic knowledge, practical skills, and personal attributes that enable them to facilitate constructive dialogue and resolution. Comprehensive training programs provide the theoretical education, practical exercises, and supervised practice needed to develop these skills. Ongoing education and certification ensure that mediators maintain high standards of practice and stay current with the latest developments in the field. By investing in the qualifications and training of mediators, we can ensure that restorative justice processes are conducted with professionalism, empathy, and effectiveness, ultimately contributing to the healing and reconciliation of all parties involved.

Skills and Techniques

Mediators are pivotal to the success of victim-offender mediation and other restorative justice processes. They employ a range of skills and techniques to facilitate productive dialogue, manage conflicts, and create a safe and supportive environment for all participants. This chapter delves into the essential skills and techniques that mediators must master, including active listening, empathy, impartiality, conflict management, and more. By honing these abilities, mediators can effectively guide participants toward meaningful resolution and healing.

Active Listening

Active listening is a fundamental skill for mediators, allowing them to fully understand and respond to the needs and concerns of all participants. It involves more than just hearing words; it requires genuine engagement and comprehension of the underlying emotions and messages.

Components of Active Listening:

1. Paying Attention: Mediators must focus completely on the speaker, avoiding distractions and demonstrating attentiveness through body language, such as nodding and maintaining eye contact.

2. Reflecting and Paraphrasing: Reflecting back what the speaker has said and paraphrasing their statements helps confirm understanding and shows the speaker that their message has been heard accurately.

3. Clarifying and Summarizing: Asking clarifying questions and summarizing key points ensures that any ambiguities are addressed and that the mediator fully grasps the speaker's perspective.

4. Non-Verbal Communication: Paying attention to non-verbal cues, such as tone of voice, facial expressions, and body language, provides additional insight into the speaker's emotions and intentions.

Benefits of Active Listening:

- Building Trust: Demonstrates respect and validation, building trust between the mediator and participants.

- Enhancing Understanding: Helps uncover underlying issues and emotions, leading to a deeper understanding of the conflict.

- Promoting Open Dialogue: Encourages participants to share openly, knowing they are being genuinely listened to.

Empathy

Empathy is the ability to understand and share the feelings of others. For mediators, empathy is crucial in creating a compassionate and supportive environment that fosters healing and reconciliation.

Practicing Empathy:

1. Emotional Awareness: Mediators must be aware of their own emotions and those of the participants. This awareness allows them to respond appropriately and sensitively.

2. Perspective-Taking: Putting themselves in the shoes of each participant helps mediators understand different viewpoints and the impact of the conflict on each individual.

3. Expressing Understanding: Verbal and non-verbal expressions of understanding and compassion, such as acknowledging feelings and providing supportive gestures, reinforce empathy.

Benefits of Empathy:

- Creating a Safe Space: Empathy helps create a safe and non-judgmental space where participants feel understood and supported.

- Facilitating Healing: Understanding the emotional experiences of participants promotes healing and emotional release.

- Building Connection: Empathy fosters connection and mutual respect, paving the way for constructive dialogue and resolution.

Impartiality

Impartiality is a cornerstone of effective mediation. Mediators must remain neutral and unbiased, ensuring that all participants feel treated fairly and equally.

Maintaining Impartiality:

1. Avoiding Judgment: Mediators must refrain from making judgments about the participants or the conflict. Their role is to facilitate dialogue, not to pass judgment.

2. Equal Treatment: Ensuring that all participants have an equal opportunity to speak and share their perspectives is crucial. Mediators must be attentive to power dynamics and strive to balance participation.

3. Transparency: Being transparent about the mediation process and their role helps mediators maintain trust and impartiality.

Benefits of Impartiality:

- Building Trust: Impartiality builds trust in the mediator and the process, encouraging participants to engage fully and openly.

- Ensuring Fairness: A neutral stance ensures that the process is fair and that all voices are heard and respected.

- Facilitating Resolution: Impartiality helps mediators guide participants toward mutually acceptable solutions without bias.

Conflict Management

Conflict management is a critical skill for mediators, enabling them to handle disputes and tensions constructively. Effective conflict management involves identifying the root causes of conflict, addressing underlying issues, and guiding participants toward resolution.

Techniques for Conflict Management:

1. Identifying Issues: Mediators must identify the key issues and interests underlying the conflict. This involves active listening and asking probing questions to uncover the core concerns.

2. De-escalation: Techniques such as taking breaks, using calming language, and redirecting focus can help de-escalate heightened emotions and prevent conflicts from escalating.

3. Facilitating Problem-Solving: Encouraging collaborative problem-solving helps participants work together to find solutions that address their needs and interests.

4. Addressing Power Imbalances: Mediators must be mindful of power dynamics and take steps to ensure that all participants have an equal voice and influence in the process.

Benefits of Conflict Management:

- Preventing Escalation: Effective conflict management prevents disputes from escalating and becoming more entrenched.

- Promoting Constructive Dialogue: Facilitating open and respectful dialogue helps participants address their differences constructively.

- Achieving Resolution: By addressing underlying issues and guiding problem-solving, mediators help participants reach mutually acceptable resolutions.

Creating a Safe and Supportive Environment

Creating a safe and supportive environment is essential for successful mediation. Participants must feel secure and respected to engage openly and honestly in the process.

Establishing Safety:

1. Setting Ground Rules: Establishing clear ground rules for the mediation process helps ensure respectful and constructive interactions. Common rules include speaking one at a time, avoiding personal attacks, and maintaining confidentiality.

2. Physical and Emotional Safety: Ensuring a comfortable and private setting, free from distractions, helps participants feel physically and emotionally safe.

3. Confidentiality: Emphasizing the confidentiality of the mediation process reassures participants that their discussions will remain private and encourages openness.

Providing Support:

1. Emotional Support: Mediators provide emotional support by acknowledging feelings, offering empathy, and validating experiences. This support helps participants feel heard and understood.

2. Guidance and Encouragement: Providing guidance and encouragement throughout the process helps participants stay focused and engaged. Mediators can offer reassurance and reinforce the importance of the process.

Benefits of a Safe and Supportive Environment:

- Encouraging Participation: A safe and supportive environment encourages all participants to engage fully and share their perspectives.

- Building Trust: Creating a secure space fosters trust in the mediator and the process, which is essential for successful mediation.

- Facilitating Healing: Participants are more likely to experience emotional healing and reconciliation in a supportive environment.

Additional Skills and Techniques

In addition to the core skills of active listening, empathy, impartiality, conflict management, and creating a safe environment, mediators employ a range of additional skills and techniques to facilitate productive mediation.

Questioning Techniques:

1. Open-Ended Questions: Asking open-ended questions encourages participants to elaborate on their thoughts and feelings, providing deeper insights into the issues at hand.

2. Clarifying Questions: Clarifying questions help ensure that the mediator understands the participants' perspectives accurately and addresses any ambiguities.

Reframing:

1. Reframing Statements: Reframing involves restating negative or contentious statements in a more neutral or positive manner. This technique can help shift the focus from blame to problem-solving.

2. Positive Spin: Highlighting positive aspects of participants' statements and actions can foster a more constructive and optimistic atmosphere.

Summarizing:

1. Periodic Summaries: Summarizing key points periodically helps keep the discussion on track and ensures

that all participants have a clear understanding of the progress made.

2. Final Summaries: Providing a final summary at the end of the session helps consolidate the discussion and sets the stage for developing agreements.

Facilitation Skills:

1. Managing Dynamics: Mediators must manage group dynamics, ensuring that all participants have an opportunity to speak and that no one dominates the discussion.

2. Encouraging Cooperation: Encouraging cooperation and collaboration helps participants work together toward mutually beneficial solutions.

Creativity and Flexibility:

1. Creative Problem-Solving: Mediators often need to think creatively to help participants develop innovative solutions to complex problems.

2. Flexibility: Flexibility is crucial in adapting to the needs and dynamics of each mediation session, ensuring that the process remains responsive and effective.

Conclusion

Mediators employ a wide range of skills and techniques to facilitate productive dialogue, manage conflicts, and create a safe and supportive environment for all participants. Active listening, empathy, impartiality, conflict management, and creating a secure space are foundational skills that enable mediators to guide participants toward meaningful resolution and healing. Additional techniques such as questioning, reframing, summarizing, and managing group dynamics further enhance the effectiveness of the mediation process. By mastering these skills and techniques, mediators can ensure that restorative justice processes are conducted with professionalism, compassion, and effectiveness, ultimately contributing to the healing and reconciliation of all parties involved.

Ethical Considerations and Challenges

Mediators play a pivotal role in the restorative justice process, and their work is guided by a set of ethical considerations and professional standards that ensure the integrity and effectiveness of the mediation process. These ethical principles address various challenges that mediators face, such as maintaining confidentiality, managing power imbalances, and ensuring voluntary participation. This chapter explores the key ethical considerations and challenges mediators encounter and provides strategies for navigating these complexities to uphold the integrity of the restorative justice process.

Maintaining Confidentiality

Confidentiality is a cornerstone of the mediation process. It ensures that participants feel safe to share their thoughts and feelings openly, knowing that their disclosures will not be shared outside the mediation session.

Principles of Confidentiality:

1. Privacy: Mediators must ensure that all discussions during the mediation process remain private and are not disclosed to outside parties without the participant's consent.

2. Trust: Maintaining confidentiality helps build trust between the mediator and the participants, which is essential for open and honest communication.

Challenges in Maintaining Confidentiality:

1. Legal Requirements: In some cases, mediators may be legally required to disclose certain information, such as when there is a risk of harm to oneself or others. Mediators must navigate these legal requirements while maintaining as much confidentiality as possible.

2. Participant Understanding: Ensuring that all participants fully understand the confidentiality rules and their exceptions can be challenging, particularly if there are language barriers or differing levels of comprehension.

Strategies for Maintaining Confidentiality:

1. Clear Communication: Mediators should clearly explain the confidentiality rules at the outset of the mediation process, including any legal exceptions.

2. Written Agreements: Having participants sign a confidentiality agreement can help reinforce the importance of maintaining privacy and provide a reference point if questions arise.

3. Secure Records: Mediators should securely store any notes or records from the mediation sessions to prevent unauthorized access.

Managing Power Imbalances

Power imbalances between participants can pose significant challenges in the mediation process. Mediators must be vigilant in identifying and addressing these imbalances to ensure that all parties can participate fully and fairly.

Identifying Power Imbalances:

1. Social and Economic Status: Differences in social and economic status can create power imbalances, with one party potentially feeling less empowered or influential.

2. Communication Skills: Variations in communication skills, such as language proficiency or confidence in speaking, can also create imbalances.

3. Psychological Factors: Trauma, fear, or intimidation can affect participants' ability to engage equally in the mediation process.

Challenges in Managing Power Imbalances:

1. Subtle Dynamics: Power imbalances can be subtle and difficult to identify, requiring mediators to be perceptive and sensitive to participants' behaviors and interactions.

2. Participant Reluctance: Participants may be reluctant to acknowledge or address power imbalances, either because they are unaware of them or because they fear repercussions.

Strategies for Managing Power Imbalances:

1. Equal Participation: Mediators should encourage equal participation by giving each party ample opportunity to speak and ensuring that no one dominates the conversation.

2. Empowerment Techniques: Techniques such as active listening, validation, and providing support can help empower less dominant participants and balance the power dynamics.

3. Separate Sessions: In some cases, holding separate sessions with each participant can help address power imbalances and prepare them for more balanced joint sessions.

Ensuring Voluntary Participation

Voluntary participation is a fundamental principle of restorative justice. It ensures that all parties are willing participants in the process and are more likely to engage meaningfully and constructively.

Principles of Voluntary Participation:

1. Consent: Participation must be based on informed consent, with all parties understanding the process and agreeing to participate freely.

2. Autonomy: Respecting participants' autonomy means recognizing their right to withdraw from the process at any time without facing negative consequences.

Challenges in Ensuring Voluntary Participation:

1. Coercion or Pressure: Participants may feel coerced or pressured to participate by external factors, such as legal requirements, social pressures, or expectations from authority figures.

2. Misunderstandings: Misunderstandings about the nature and purpose of the mediation process can affect participants' willingness to engage voluntarily.

Strategies for Ensuring Voluntary Participation:

1. Informed Consent: Mediators should provide comprehensive information about the mediation process, including its goals, procedures, and potential outcomes, to ensure that participants can make an informed decision.

2. Creating a Safe Environment: Creating a supportive and non-judgmental environment helps participants feel more comfortable and willing to engage voluntarily.

3. Respecting Autonomy: Mediators must respect participants' decisions to withdraw from the process if they choose to do so and should ensure that this option is always available.

Navigating Ethical Dilemmas

Mediators often face ethical dilemmas that require careful consideration and judgment. Navigating these dilemmas involves balancing the interests of all parties while adhering to ethical principles and professional standards.

Common Ethical Dilemmas:

1. Conflict of Interest: Mediators may encounter situations where there is a potential conflict of interest, such as personal relationships with participants or prior involvement in related matters.

2. Confidentiality vs. Duty to Warn: Mediators may need to balance confidentiality with the duty to warn if there is a risk of harm to oneself or others.

3. Impartiality Challenges: Maintaining impartiality can be challenging if the mediator has strong feelings about the case or if there are significant power imbalances.

Strategies for Navigating Ethical Dilemmas:

1. Ethical Guidelines: Adhering to established ethical guidelines and professional standards provides a framework for navigating ethical dilemmas.

2. Supervision and Consultation: Seeking supervision or consultation from experienced mediators or ethics committees can provide valuable insights and support in resolving ethical dilemmas.

3. Reflective Practice: Regular reflective practice helps mediators critically examine their own actions and decisions, fostering ethical awareness and continuous improvement.

Professional Standards and Guidelines

Adhering to professional standards and guidelines is essential for maintaining the integrity and effectiveness of the mediation process. These standards provide a benchmark for ethical practice and ensure that mediators uphold the highest levels of professionalism.

Key Professional Standards:

1. Competence: Mediators must possess the necessary skills, knowledge, and qualifications to conduct effective mediation. This includes ongoing professional development and training.

2. Impartiality: Mediators must remain neutral and impartial, ensuring that all parties are treated fairly and equally.

3. Confidentiality: Mediators must maintain confidentiality and ensure that all information disclosed during the mediation process is kept private, except in cases where disclosure is legally required.

4. Voluntariness: Participation in mediation must be voluntary, with all parties providing informed consent and having the freedom to withdraw at any time.

Importance of Certification:

1. Professional Credibility: Certification from recognized professional organizations enhances the credibility and legitimacy of mediators, demonstrating their commitment to ethical practice and professional standards.

2. Ongoing Development: Certification often requires ongoing education and training, ensuring that mediators stay current with the latest developments and best practices in the field.

Conclusion

Mediators face numerous ethical considerations and challenges in their role, including maintaining confidentiality, managing power imbalances, ensuring voluntary participation, and navigating ethical dilemmas. Adhering to ethical guidelines and professional standards is crucial for upholding the integrity of the mediation process and fostering trust among participants. By being aware of these ethical considerations and employing strategies to address them, mediators can effectively guide participants toward meaningful resolution and healing. Continuous professional development and adherence to certification requirements further ensure that mediators maintain high standards of practice and contribute to the overall effectiveness of restorative justice processes.

CHAPTER 05

CASE STUDIES IN VICTIM-OFFENDER MEDIATION

Success Stories

Success stories in victim-offender mediation highlight the transformative potential of restorative justice practices. These real-life examples demonstrate how individuals and communities can heal, rebuild, and grow through the mediation process. By examining these cases, practitioners and policymakers can gain valuable insights into the effectiveness of restorative justice and the practical applications of its principles. This chapter presents several success stories that illustrate the profound impact of victim-offender mediation on victims, offenders, and communities.

Case Study 1: Healing After Burglary

Background:

In a small suburban community, a young man named Tom broke into a family's home, stealing valuables and causing significant emotional distress. The victims, a couple with two young children, were traumatized by the invasion of their private space and the loss of sentimental items.

Mediation Process:

1. Initial Contact: The victims were initially hesitant but agreed to participate in mediation after understanding its potential benefits. Tom also expressed remorse and a willingness to make amends.

2. Preparation: Separate preparatory meetings were held with Tom and the victims. These sessions helped build trust and readiness for the joint mediation session.

3. Mediation Session: During the mediation, Tom apologized sincerely and explained the circumstances that led to his actions, including his struggle with addiction. The victims shared the emotional impact of the burglary on their family, expressing their fears and anxieties.

4. Reparation Agreement: The mediation resulted in a reparation agreement where Tom committed to participating in a rehabilitation program and performing community service. He also agreed to work towards compensating the family for the stolen items.

Outcome:

1. Victims' Perspective: The victims reported feeling a sense of closure and relief after hearing Tom's apology and understanding his situation. The process helped them regain a sense of security and trust.

2. Offender's Perspective: Tom felt a profound sense of accountability and relief after the mediation. The agreement provided him with a clear path to rehabilitation and reintegration into the community.

3. Community Impact: The community saw a reduction in similar crimes as the mediation process was publicized, highlighting the benefits of restorative justice. Tom's involvement in community service also helped rebuild trust within the neighborhood.

Case Study 2: Restoring Harmony in a School

Background:

In high school, a conflict between two students, Sarah and Emily, escalated into a physical altercation. The incident disrupted the school environment, creating tension among students and staff.

Mediation Process:

1. Initial Contact: Both students and their parents were approached by the school's restorative justice coordinator. After some initial resistance, they agreed to participate in mediation.

2. Preparation: The coordinator held separate meetings with Sarah, Emily, and their families to prepare them for the mediation session. These meetings helped clarify expectations and address any concerns.

. Mediation Session: During the mediation, Sarah and Emily shared their perspectives on the conflict. They discussed the events that led to the altercation and the feelings of hurt and anger. Facilitated by the coordinator, they explored underlying issues such as peer pressure and miscommunication.

4. Restorative Agreement: The session concluded with a restorative agreement. Both students agreed to participate in peer mediation training and to collaborate on a project promoting positive school culture. They also committed to regular check-ins with the coordinator.

Outcome:

1. Students' Perspective: Sarah and Emily reported feeling understood and respected after the mediation. The process helped them rebuild their relationship and develop conflict-resolution skills.

2. School Environment: The school experienced a significant improvement in the overall environment. The mediation not only resolved the immediate conflict but also

promoted a culture of empathy and cooperation among students.

3. Community Impact: The success of the mediation encouraged the school to adopt restorative practices more broadly, leading to a decrease in disciplinary incidents and fostering a more supportive educational community.

Case Study 3: Reconciliation After a Violent Crime

Background:

In a rural town, a violent altercation between two neighbors, Mark and John, resulted in serious injuries to John. The incident caused deep divisions within the community, with residents taking sides and the sense of unity being severely damaged.

Mediation Process:

1. Initial Contact: Initially, both Mark and John were reluctant to participate in mediation. However, with encouragement from community leaders and the realization of the potential benefits, they agreed.

2. Preparation: The mediator conducted extensive preparatory sessions with Mark, John, and their families to address fears and build readiness for the mediation.

3. Mediation Session: The mediation was intense, with both parties expressing deep-seated anger and resentment. Through guided dialogue, they began to explore the root

causes of their conflict, which included misunderstandings and long-standing grievances.

4. Reparation Agreement: The mediation resulted in a comprehensive reparation agreement. Mark agreed to cover John's medical expenses and to perform community service. Both parties also agreed to participate in community reconciliation activities to help mend the broader rift.

Outcome:

1. Victim's Perspective: John expressed relief and a sense of closure after the mediation. Understanding Mark's perspective and receiving a sincere apology helped him begin the healing process.

2. Offender's Perspective: Mark felt a deep sense of accountability and a commitment to making amends. The process provided him with a constructive way to address the harm he had caused.

3. Community Impact: The mediation had a ripple effect on the community, promoting healing and reconciliation. The community activities helped restore trust and unity, demonstrating the power of restorative justice in resolving even the most serious conflicts.

Case Study 4: Transforming a Workplace Conflict

Background:

In a mid-sized company, a conflict between two employees, Maria and James, over workplace responsibilities and communication styles led to a toxic work environment. The ongoing tension affected team morale and productivity.

Mediation Process:

1. Initial Contact: The human resources department suggested mediation, and both Maria and James agreed, recognizing the need for resolution.

2. Preparation: The mediator held separate sessions with Maria and James to understand their perspectives and prepare them for the joint session. This preparation helped build trust and set the stage for constructive dialogue.

3. Mediation Session: During the mediation, Maria and James discussed the specific incidents that had caused friction. The mediator facilitated a discussion on their communication styles and work expectations, helping them understand each other's viewpoints.

4. Restorative Agreement: The mediation concluded with a restorative agreement where both parties agreed to regular check-ins, improved communication strategies, and participation in team-building activities. They also agreed to provide mutual feedback in a constructive manner.

Outcome:

1. Employees' Perspective: Maria and James reported improved communication and a better understanding of each other's work styles. The mediation process helped them rebuild trust and collaborate more effectively.

2. Work Environment: The overall work environment improved significantly, with increased team morale and productivity. The successful mediation also encouraged the company to adopt restorative practices more broadly in handling workplace conflicts.

3. Organizational Impact: The company benefited from reduced turnover and a more cohesive team, demonstrating the value of restorative justice in enhancing workplace relationships and productivity.

Conclusion

These success stories illustrate the transformative potential of victim-offender mediation and restorative justice practices. By providing a platform for open dialogue, accountability, and healing, these processes help individuals and communities move beyond conflict and rebuild trust. For practitioners and policymakers, these cases offer valuable insights into the practical applications of restorative justice and its profound impact on resolving conflicts, promoting reconciliation, and fostering a more supportive and cohesive community. As restorative justice practices continue to evolve and expand, the lessons learned from these success stories will play a crucial role in guiding future efforts and enhancing the effectiveness of mediation processes.

Lessons Learned

Analyzing case studies in victim-offender mediation not only highlights successes but also reveals valuable lessons and areas for improvement. By understanding what works and what doesn't, practitioners can refine their approaches and enhance the effectiveness of mediation processes. This chapter examines the lessons learned from various case studies, focusing on preparation, process, follow-up, and overall effectiveness. These insights provide practical guidance for mediators and policymakers striving to improve restorative justice practices.

Importance of Thorough Preparation

One of the most critical lessons learned from successful mediation is the importance of thorough preparation. Effective preparation sets the foundation for a constructive and meaningful mediation process.

Key Takeaways:

1. Building Trust: Establishing trust between mediators and participants during the preparatory phase is crucial. Initial meetings should focus on building rapport, addressing concerns, and setting expectations.

2. Understanding Perspectives: Mediators must take the time to understand the backgrounds, needs, and perspectives of all participants. This understanding helps tailor the mediation process to address specific issues and dynamics.

3. Clear Communication: Providing clear and comprehensive information about the mediation process, including its goals, procedures, and potential outcomes, ensures that participants are well-informed and ready to engage.

Areas for Improvement:

1. More Comprehensive Screening: Implementing more comprehensive screening procedures to assess suitability for mediation can help identify potential challenges and prepare participants more effectively.

2. Enhanced Support Services: Offering additional support services, such as counseling or legal advice, during the preparatory phase can help participants feel more secure and supported.

Effective Facilitation Techniques

Effective facilitation techniques are essential for guiding the mediation process and ensuring productive dialogue. Successful mediators employ a range of strategies to manage conflicts, foster empathy, and facilitate resolution.

Key Takeaways:

1. Active Listening: Mediators who practice active listening, reflecting back what participants say and validating their feelings, create a safe and respectful environment that encourages open dialogue.

2. Empathy and Neutrality: Demonstrating empathy while maintaining neutrality helps mediators build trust and facilitate constructive interactions between participants.

3. Managing Emotions: Skilled mediators use techniques to manage emotions, such as de-escalation strategies and taking breaks, to prevent conflicts from escalating and to maintain a productive atmosphere.

Areas for Improvement:

1. Ongoing Training: Continuous training and professional development for mediators in advanced facilitation techniques can enhance their skills and effectiveness.

2. Adapting Techniques: Being adaptable and flexible in applying different facilitation techniques to suit the specific needs and dynamics of each case can improve outcomes.

Addressing Power Imbalances

Power imbalances between participants can significantly impact the mediation process. Effective strategies to address these imbalances are essential for ensuring fairness and equal participation.

Key Takeaways:

1. Identifying Imbalances: Early identification of power imbalances allows mediators to implement strategies to address them, such as ensuring equal speaking time and providing additional support to less dominant participants.

2. Empowerment Techniques: Using empowerment techniques, such as active listening and validation, helps balance power dynamics and encourages less dominant participants to engage fully.

3. Separate Sessions: Holding separate preparatory sessions with each participant can help address power imbalances and prepare them for balanced joint sessions.

Areas for Improvement:

1. More Robust Assessment: Developing more robust assessment tools to identify power imbalances early in the process can help mediators implement appropriate strategies more effectively.

2. Additional Resources: Providing additional resources and support, such as advocacy services, can help empower participants who may feel marginalized or less powerful.

Ensuring Voluntary Participation

Ensuring voluntary participation is a fundamental principle of restorative justice. Participants who engage willingly are more likely to contribute meaningfully to the mediation process and achieve positive outcomes.

Key Takeaways:

1. Informed Consent: Clear communication about the mediation process and obtaining informed consent from all participants ensures that they understand and agree to the process voluntarily.

2. Respecting Autonomy: Respecting participants' autonomy and their right to withdraw from the process at any time fosters a sense of control and trust in the mediation process.

3. Creating a Safe Environment: A safe and non-judgmental environment encourages participants to engage voluntarily and openly.

Areas for Improvement:

1. Enhanced Communication: Improving communication strategies to ensure that all participants fully understand the process and their rights can enhance voluntary participation.

2. Continuous Reassessment: Continuously reassessing participants' willingness to engage throughout the

mediation process can help address any emerging concerns or reservations.

Importance of Follow-Up and Support

Follow-up and ongoing support are critical components of the mediation process, ensuring that agreements are implemented and that participants continue to receive the support they need.

Key Takeaways:

1. Regular Check-Ins: Regular check-ins with participants help monitor progress, address challenges, and provide ongoing support, ensuring that the agreements are implemented successfully.

2. Support Services: Providing access to support services, such as counseling, legal advice, and community resources, helps participants navigate any difficulties and reinforces their commitment to the agreements.

3. Community Involvement: Involving the community in the follow-up process promotes accountability and support, helping participants reintegrate and maintain positive changes.

Areas for Improvement:

1. Structured Follow-Up Plans: Developing structured follow-up plans with clear timelines and responsibilities can enhance the effectiveness of follow-up efforts.

2. Comprehensive Support Networks: Building comprehensive support networks that include various services and resources can provide more holistic support to participants.

Evaluating and Measuring Success

Evaluating and measuring the success of mediation processes provides valuable insights into their effectiveness and areas for improvement. Continuous evaluation helps refine practices and improve outcomes.

Key Takeaways:

1. Participant Feedback: Gathering feedback from participants provides direct insights into their experiences and the impact of the mediation process. This feedback is essential for understanding what works and what needs improvement.

2. Outcome Metrics: Using quantitative metrics, such as completion rates of agreements, recidivism rates, and levels of participant satisfaction, helps measure the effectiveness of mediation processes.

3. Qualitative Insights: Collecting qualitative insights through participant narratives and case studies provides a deeper understanding of the personal and relational transformations that occur through mediation.

Areas for Improvement:

1.   Comprehensive Evaluation Frameworks: Developing comprehensive evaluation frameworks that combine quantitative and qualitative data can provide a more holistic understanding of the success and impact of mediation processes.

2.   Continuous Improvement: Using evaluation findings to continuously improve mediation practices and processes ensures that restorative justice remains responsive and effective.

Conclusion

Analyzing case studies in victim-offender mediation reveals valuable lessons and areas for improvement that can enhance the effectiveness of restorative justice practices. Thorough preparation, effective facilitation techniques, addressing power imbalances, ensuring voluntary participation, and providing follow-up and support are all critical components of successful mediation. Continuous evaluation and the use of participant feedback further refine these practices, ensuring that restorative justice processes are conducted with professionalism, empathy, and effectiveness. By learning from these lessons, practitioners and policymakers can improve the quality and impact of mediation processes, ultimately contributing to the healing and reconciliation of all parties involved.

Critical Analysis

A critical analysis of case studies in victim-offender mediation provides an in-depth examination of outcomes, identifies patterns, and assesses the overall impact of restorative justice practices. This analysis is crucial for building a robust evidence base, refining mediation techniques, and informing future practice and policy development. By critically evaluating these case studies, we can understand the strengths and limitations of current approaches and make data-driven recommendations for improvement.

Examining Outcomes

A thorough examination of the outcomes of victim-offender mediation helps assess the effectiveness of these processes in achieving their intended goals. Key outcomes to evaluate include victim satisfaction, offender accountability, community impact, and long-term benefits.

Victim Satisfaction:

1. Emotional Healing: Assess the extent to which victims experience emotional healing and closure through the mediation process. This can be measured through post-mediation surveys and interviews.

2. Sense of Justice: Evaluate whether victims feel that justice has been served and their needs have been addressed.

This includes their satisfaction with the reparation agreements and the offender's accountability.

3. Empowerment: Determine whether victims feel empowered and supported throughout the mediation process. This involves assessing their level of participation and their perceptions of being heard and respected.

Offender Accountability:

1. Acknowledgment of Harm: Assess whether offenders genuinely acknowledge the harm they have caused and express remorse. This can be evaluated through their statements and actions during and after the mediation.

2. Commitment to Change: Evaluate the extent to which offenders commit to making amends and changing their behavior. This includes their compliance with reparation agreements and engagement in rehabilitation programs.

3. Reduced Recidivism: Measure the impact of mediation on reducing recidivism rates among offenders. This involves tracking their behavior over time and comparing it with those who did not participate in mediation.

Community Impact:

1. Restored Relationships: Assess the extent to which mediation helps restore relationships within the community. This includes the reintegration of offenders and the healing of community divisions.

2. Enhanced Social Cohesion: Evaluate the overall impact of mediation on community cohesion and trust. This involves measuring changes in community attitudes and behaviors toward conflict resolution.

3. Preventive Effects: Determine whether the mediation process has preventive effects, such as reducing the likelihood of future conflicts and promoting a culture of accountability and reconciliation.

Long-Term Benefits:

1. Sustained Change: Assess the long-term impact of mediation on both victims and offenders. This includes evaluating their well-being, personal growth and continued engagement in positive behaviors.

2. Ongoing Support: Evaluate the effectiveness of follow-up and support services in maintaining the benefits of mediation. This involves assessing the availability and utilization of support resources.

Identifying Patterns

Identifying patterns in case studies helps uncover common factors that contribute to successful outcomes and highlight areas that require attention. This analysis can inform best practices and guide the development of effective mediation programs.

Factors Contributing to Success:

1. Effective Preparation: Successful mediations often involve thorough preparation, including building trust, understanding perspectives, and addressing concerns before the joint session.

2. Skilled Facilitation: The role of skilled mediators who use active listening, empathy, impartiality, and conflict management techniques is crucial in guiding productive dialogue and resolution.

3. Balanced Power Dynamics: Addressing power imbalances effectively ensures that all participants can engage fully and fairly in the mediation process.

4. Voluntary Participation: Ensuring that participation is voluntary and based on informed consent enhances the likelihood of meaningful engagement and positive outcomes.

Common Challenges:

1. Emotional Barriers: Emotional barriers, such as anger, fear, and trauma, can hinder the mediation process. Identifying strategies to address and manage these emotions is essential for success.

2. Power Imbalances: Power imbalances between participants can create challenges in achieving fair and equitable outcomes. Effective strategies to balance power dynamics are critical.

3. Lack of Follow-Up: Inadequate follow-up and support can undermine the long-term effectiveness of mediation agreements. Ensuring ongoing support is vital for sustained change.

Areas for Improvement:

1. Enhanced Screening: Implementing more comprehensive screening procedures to assess suitability for mediation and identify potential challenges early in the process.

2. Additional Training: Providing ongoing training and professional development for mediators in advanced facilitation techniques, cultural sensitivity, and trauma-informed approaches.

3. Structured Follow-Up: Develop structured follow-up plans with clear timelines and responsibilities to ensure the effective implementation of mediation agreements and continued support for participants.

Assessing Overall Impact

Assessing the overall impact of victim-offender mediation involves evaluating its broader implications for restorative justice practices, policy development, and community well-being.

Evidence Base for Restorative Justice:

1. Research and Data Collection: Collecting and analyzing data from case studies contributes to the evidence base for restorative justice. This includes quantitative metrics, such as recidivism rates and victim satisfaction, as well as qualitative insights from participant narratives.

2. Comparative Studies: Conducting comparative studies that examine the outcomes of mediation versus traditional justice approaches provides valuable insights into the effectiveness and benefits of restorative justice.

3. Longitudinal Studies: Longitudinal studies that track participants over time offer a comprehensive understanding of the long-term impact of mediation on individuals and communities.

Policy Development:

1. Informed Policy Making: Critical analysis of case studies informs policy development by highlighting best practices, identifying challenges, and providing evidence-based recommendations for improving restorative justice programs.

2. Resource Allocation: Understanding the factors that contribute to successful mediation helps policymakers allocate resources effectively, ensuring that mediation programs receive the support they need to thrive.

3. Legislative Support: Advocacy for legislative support and funding for restorative justice programs is strengthened by robust data and success stories from case studies.

Community Well-Being:

1. Enhanced Social Fabric: The overall impact of mediation on community well-being includes improved social cohesion, reduced conflict, and a stronger sense of trust and cooperation among community members.

2. Preventive Benefits: Restorative justice practices have preventive benefits, such as reducing the likelihood of future conflicts and promoting a culture of accountability and reconciliation.

3. Empowered Communities: Communities that embrace restorative justice practices are often more empowered to address conflicts constructively and support the healing and growth of their members.

Conclusion

A critical analysis of case studies in victim-offender mediation provides valuable insights into the effectiveness and impact of restorative justice practices. By examining outcomes, identifying patterns, and assessing the overall impact, practitioners and policymakers can refine their approaches, enhance the effectiveness of mediation processes, and build a robust evidence base for restorative justice. These insights contribute to informed policy development, improved resource allocation, and the promotion of community well-being. As restorative justice practices continue to evolve, ongoing critical analysis will play a crucial role in ensuring their success and sustainability, ultimately contributing to a more just and compassionate society.

CHAPTER 06

PSYCHOLOGICAL AND EMOTIONAL IMPACT

Healing Trauma

Victim-offender mediation can be a powerful tool for healing trauma for both victims and offenders. The structured, supportive environment of mediation allows individuals to confront their trauma, facilitating emotional release and closure. This chapter explores how the mediation process aids in healing trauma, providing pathways for victims to regain control and for offenders to experience catharsis and personal growth.

Understanding Trauma

Trauma is an emotional response to a deeply distressing or disturbing event. It can have long-lasting psychological effects, impacting a person's ability to function and their overall well-being. Trauma can manifest in various ways, including anxiety, depression, flashbacks, and emotional numbness.

Types of Trauma:

1. Acute Trauma: Resulting from a single incident, such as a violent crime or accident.

2. Chronic Trauma: Stemming from repeated and prolonged experiences, such as domestic violence or abuse.

3. Complex Trauma: Involving exposure to multiple traumatic events, often of an invasive, interpersonal nature.

Effects of Trauma:

1. Emotional Effects: Including feelings of fear, anger, sadness, and shame.

2. Psychological Effects: Such as post-traumatic stress disorder (PTSD), depression, and anxiety.

3. Physical Effects: Including headaches, fatigue, and other stress-related symptoms.

4. Behavioral Effects: Such as withdrawal, aggression, or substance abuse.

Healing Trauma Through Mediation

Victim-offender mediation provides a unique opportunity for healing by addressing the emotional and psychological needs of both victims and offenders. The process creates a safe space for confronting trauma and facilitates healing through structured dialogue and support.

For Victims:

1. Confronting Trauma:

- Narrative Control: Mediation allows victims to tell their story in their own words, which can be empowering and validating. This narrative control helps them reclaim their identity and sense of agency.

- Emotional Release: Sharing their experiences and emotions in a supportive environment provides victims with an opportunity for emotional release, which is essential for healing.

2. Receiving Acknowledgment:

- Validation: Hearing the offender acknowledge the harm and express remorse can validate the victim's experiences and emotions, contributing to their healing.

- Answers and Understanding: Mediation provides a platform for victims to ask questions and gain understanding about the offender's motives and circumstances, which can help resolve lingering doubts and fears.

3. Achieving Closure:

- Restitution Agreements: Developing restitution agreements that address the victim's needs helps provide a sense of justice and closure.

- Empowerment: Active participation in the mediation process empowers victims, helping them move from a position of helplessness to one of control and influence over the resolution of their trauma.

For Offenders:

1. Acknowledging Harm:

- Confronting Impact: Mediation requires offenders to confront the impact of their actions on victims, which can lead to genuine remorse and accountability.

- Emotional Catharsis: Expressing remorse and making amends can provide a form of emotional catharsis for offenders, helping them release guilt and shame.

2. Personal Growth:

- Empathy Development: Hearing the victim's story and understanding their pain can foster empathy in offenders, contributing to their personal growth and rehabilitation.

- Commitment to Change: The mediation process encourages offenders to commit to positive change, promoting behaviors that prevent future harm and support their reintegration into society.

3. Healing Relationships:

- Reconciliation: Mediation can help offenders repair relationships with victims, their own families, and the broader community, facilitating their healing and reintegration.

- Supportive Networks: Through mediation, offenders can build supportive networks that assist them in maintaining positive changes and avoiding recidivism.

The Role of Mediators in Healing Trauma

Mediators play a crucial role in facilitating the healing of trauma during the mediation process. Their skills and techniques are vital in creating a safe and supportive environment, managing emotions, and guiding constructive dialogue.

Creating a Safe Environment:

1. Establishing Trust: Building trust with participants from the outset is essential. Mediators must demonstrate empathy, neutrality, and professionalism to create a safe space.

2. Setting Ground Rules: Establishing clear ground rules for respectful communication and confidentiality helps participants feel secure and respected.

3. Providing Emotional Support: Mediators offer emotional support through active listening, validation, and reassurance, helping participants manage their emotions during the process.

Managing Emotions:

1. De-escalation Techniques: Mediators use de-escalation techniques, such as taking breaks and redirecting

focus, to manage intense emotions and prevent conflicts from escalating.

2. Acknowledging Feelings: Validating participants' feelings and acknowledging their pain and suffering is crucial for emotional healing.

3. Facilitating Emotional Expression: Encouraging participants to express their emotions constructively helps them process their trauma and move toward healing.

Guiding Constructive Dialogue:

1. Active Listening: Mediators practice active listening to ensure that participants feel heard and understood, which is essential for building trust and facilitating dialogue.

2. Empathy and Neutrality: Demonstrating empathy while maintaining neutrality helps mediators foster a supportive environment where participants can engage openly and honestly.

3. Encouraging Mutual Understanding: Mediators guide participants in exploring each other's perspectives and experiences, promoting empathy and mutual understanding.

Challenges in Healing Trauma Through Mediation

While victim-offender mediation can be a powerful tool for healing trauma, it also presents challenges that mediators must navigate to ensure its effectiveness.

Emotional Intensity:

1. Managing Intense Emotions: Participants may experience intense emotions, such as anger, fear, or grief, which can be challenging to manage. Mediators must be skilled in handling these emotions constructively.

2. Avoiding Re-traumatization: It is essential to avoid re-traumatizing participants by ensuring that the process is sensitive and supportive. Mediators must be aware of trauma triggers and take steps to mitigate them.

Power Imbalances:

1. Addressing Power Dynamics: Power imbalances between victims and offenders can impact the mediation process. Mediators must be vigilant in identifying and addressing these imbalances to ensure fair and equitable participation.

2. Empowering Participants: Mediators should use empowerment techniques to support less dominant participants, helping them engage fully and confidently in the process.

Voluntary Participation:

1. Ensuring Voluntary Engagement: Participation in mediation must be voluntary and based on informed consent. Mediators must ensure that all participants understand the process and agree to participate willingly.

2. Respecting Autonomy: Mediators must respect participants' autonomy and their right to withdraw from the process if they choose to do so.

Conclusion

Victim-offender mediation provides a unique and powerful avenue for healing trauma for both victims and offenders. The process facilitates emotional release, closure, and personal growth by creating a supportive environment where individuals can confront their trauma and engage in constructive dialogue. Mediators play a crucial role in guiding this process, using their skills to manage emotions, address power imbalances, and foster mutual understanding. While challenges exist, the potential for healing and transformation through mediation is profound, offering a pathway to recovery and reconciliation for those affected by trauma. As restorative justice practices continue to evolve, the lessons learned from mediation can further enhance its effectiveness in healing trauma and promoting emotional and psychological well-being.

Building Empathy and Understanding

One of the most profound benefits of victim-offender mediation is its ability to build empathy and understanding between participants. The structured dialogue facilitated by mediators allows victims and offenders to hear each other's stories and perspectives, fostering deeper connections and reducing feelings of animosity and resentment. This chapter explores the mechanisms through which mediation fosters empathy and understanding, highlighting the transformative impact on both individuals and the broader community.

The Role of Empathy in Restorative Justice

Empathy is the ability to understand and share the feelings of another person. In the context of restorative justice, empathy plays a crucial role in healing and reconciliation. When victims and offenders develop empathy for each other, they can move beyond the roles of "victim" and "offender" and see each other as human beings with complex emotions and experiences.

Benefits of Empathy:

1. Emotional Healing: Empathy helps victims feel understood and validated, which is essential for emotional healing.

2. Reduced Recidivism: Offenders who develop empathy for their victims are more likely to change their behavior and avoid reoffending.

3. Social Cohesion: Empathy fosters a sense of community and social cohesion, reducing the likelihood of future conflicts.

Mechanisms for Building Empathy and Understanding

Victim-offender mediation employs several mechanisms to build empathy and understanding between participants. These mechanisms are facilitated by skilled mediators who create a safe and supportive environment for open dialogue.

Storytelling:

1. Sharing Experiences: Mediation provides a platform for victims and offenders to share their personal stories. Victims can express how the crime affected their lives, while offenders can explain their actions and the circumstances that led to the offense.

2. Humanizing Participants: Hearing each other's stories humanizes both victims and offenders, allowing them to see each other as individuals rather than stereotypes.

Active Listening:

1. Demonstrating Attention: Mediators practice active listening, demonstrating attention and understanding through verbal and non-verbal cues. This encourages participants to listen to each other with empathy.

2. Reflecting and Paraphrasing: Reflecting back and paraphrasing what participants say helps ensure that they feel heard and understood, fostering mutual respect.

Guided Dialogue:

1. Facilitating Questions: Mediators facilitate questions that encourage participants to explore each other's perspectives and emotions. Questions such as "How did that make you feel?" or "What was going through your mind?" promote deeper understanding.

2. Encouraging Open Communication: Mediators create an environment where participants feel safe to communicate openly, without fear of judgment or retribution.

Empathy-Building Exercises:

1. Perspective-Taking Activities: Mediators may use exercises that encourage participants to put themselves in each other's shoes, fostering empathy and understanding.

2. Shared Goals: Developing shared goals for the mediation process, such as achieving healing and reconciliation, helps participants see each other as allies rather than adversaries.

Case Studies Illustrating Empathy and Understanding

Several case studies highlight the impact of empathy and understanding in victim-offender mediation. These real-life examples demonstrate how the mediation process can transform relationships and promote healing.

Case Study 1: Restoring Family Bonds

Background:

A young man named Jake was involved in a robbery that traumatized a small business owner, Mr. Thompson. The incident strained relationships within the community and between Jake and his family.

Mediation Process:

1. Storytelling: During mediation, Mr. Thompson shared the fear and anxiety he experienced during and after the robbery. Jake, in turn, explained his desperate circumstances and poor choices.

2. Active Listening: Mediators encouraged active listening, allowing both parties to express their feelings and perspectives without interruption.

3. Perspective-Taking: Exercises that prompted Jake to imagine himself in Mr. Thompson's position helped build empathy.

Outcome:

1. Empathy Development: Jake developed a deeper understanding of the impact of his actions on Mr. Thompson and the community.

2. Healing: Mr. Thompson felt heard and validated, which facilitated his emotional healing.

3. Reconciliation: The process helped restore relationships within the community and between Jake and his family, promoting social cohesion.

Case Study 2: Bridging Generational Gaps

Background:

A conflict between a teenager, Sarah, and an elderly neighbor, Mrs. Jenkins, escalated after Sarah vandalized Mrs. Jenkins' garden. The incident created tension between different generations in the neighborhood.

Mediation Process:

1. Storytelling: Sarah shared her feelings of frustration and neglect that led to her actions. Mrs. Jenkins explained the emotional significance of her garden and the hurt caused by its destruction.

2. Empathy-Building Exercises: Mediators used exercises that encouraged Sarah to appreciate the value of the garden to Mrs. Jenkins and for Mrs. Jenkins to understand Sarah's struggles.

3. Guided Dialogue: Facilitated questions helped both parties explore each other's emotions and experiences.

Outcome:

1. Empathy Development: Both Sarah and Mrs. Jenkins developed empathy for each other, reducing animosity and resentment.

2. Reconciliation: The process fostered mutual understanding and respect, bridging the generational gap in the neighborhood.

3. Community Impact: The successful mediation encouraged other community members to engage in dialogue and empathy-building activities, promoting a more cohesive community.

Challenges in Building Empathy and Understanding

While victim-offender mediation can be highly effective in building empathy and understanding, it also presents challenges that mediators must navigate.

Emotional Barriers:

1. Intense Emotions: Participants may experience intense emotions such as anger, fear, and grief, which can hinder the development of empathy.

2. Resistance to Understanding: Some participants may initially resist understanding the other party's perspective due to deep-seated animosity or trauma.

Power Imbalances:

1. Unequal Participation: Power imbalances can affect the ability of participants to engage equally in the mediation process, hindering the development of mutual empathy.

2. Facilitating Fair Dialogue: Mediators must be skilled in managing power dynamics to ensure that all voices are heard and respected.

Cultural and Personal Differences:

1. Diverse Backgrounds: Participants may come from diverse cultural and personal backgrounds, leading to different communication styles and worldviews that can complicate the mediation process.

2. Cultural Sensitivity: Mediators must be culturally sensitive and adaptable, using techniques that respect and bridge cultural differences.

Strategies for Overcoming Challenges

Mediators can employ several strategies to overcome challenges in building empathy and understanding, ensuring a successful mediation process.

Emotional Support:

1. Providing Safe Spaces: Creating a safe and supportive environment helps participants feel secure in expressing their emotions and perspectives.

2. Validating Emotions: Acknowledging and validating participants' emotions helps reduce resistance and promote openness.

Addressing Power Imbalances:

1. Empowerment Techniques: Using empowerment techniques, such as active listening and validation, helps balance power dynamics and encourages equal participation.

2. Separate Sessions: Holding separate sessions with each participant can address power imbalances and prepare them for balanced joint sessions.

Cultural Sensitivity:

1. Cultural Competence Training: Mediators should undergo cultural competence training to better understand and navigate cultural differences.

2. Adaptable Techniques: Using adaptable mediation techniques that respect and bridge cultural differences helps ensure effective communication and understanding.

Conclusion

Victim-offender mediation has the transformative potential to build empathy and understanding between participants. By facilitating storytelling, active listening, guided dialogue, and empathy-building exercises, mediators help victims and offenders develop deeper connections and reduce feelings of animosity and resentment. Despite challenges such as emotional barriers, power imbalances, and cultural differences, effective strategies and skilled facilitation can overcome these obstacles. The resulting empathy and understanding not only promote healing and reconciliation for individuals but also foster social cohesion and a more compassionate community. As restorative justice practices continue to evolve, the emphasis on empathy and understanding will remain central to their success and impact.

Transformational Narratives

Transformational narratives are powerful stories that emerge from the mediation process, illustrating the journey from harm to healing for individuals and communities. These narratives showcase the potential for positive change and highlight the impact of restorative justice in fostering resilience and reconciliation. This chapter explores the elements of transformational narratives, their significance, and the ways in which they contribute to community healing and resilience.

The Elements of Transformational Narratives

Transformational narratives in the context of victim-offender mediation typically include several key elements that highlight the process of healing and change.

1. Acknowledgment of Harm:

Victim's Perspective:

- Expressing Pain: Victims share their experiences of harm and the impact it has had on their lives. This acknowledgment validates their suffering and begins the healing process.

- Seeking Answers: Victims often have questions about the offense and the offender's motivations. Receiving answers can help them understand and come to terms with their trauma.

Offender's Perspective:

- Taking Responsibility: Offenders acknowledge the harm they have caused, which is a critical step in demonstrating genuine remorse and accountability.

- Expressing Remorse: Offenders articulate their regret and the emotional impact of their actions, which can facilitate empathy and understanding from the victim.

2. Emotional and Psychological Healing:

Victim's Perspective:

- Emotional Release: Sharing their story in a supportive environment allows victims to release pent-up emotions, which is essential for emotional healing.

- Empowerment: Active participation in the mediation process empowers victims, helping them regain a sense of control over their lives.

Offender's Perspective:

- Catharsis: Expressing remorse and making amends can provide a cathartic release for offenders, helping them to move beyond guilt and shame.

- Personal Growth: The mediation process encourages offenders to reflect on their actions and commit to positive change, fostering personal growth.

3. Reparation and Reconciliation:

Victim's Perspective:

- Achieving Closure: Developing and agreeing to a plan for restitution helps victims achieve a sense of closure and justice.

- Rebuilding Trust: Successful mediation can help rebuild trust with the offender and within the broader community, promoting a sense of safety and belonging.

Offender's Perspective:

- Making Amends: Fulfilling the terms of the restitution agreement allows offenders to make tangible amends for their actions, contributing to their rehabilitation.

- Reintegration: The process of making amends and demonstrating change helps offenders reintegrate into the community and rebuild their lives.

4. Community Healing and Resilience:

- Shared Stories: Transformational narratives are shared within the community, promoting a collective understanding of the restorative justice process and its benefits.

- Fostering Empathy: These narratives foster empathy and understanding among community members, reducing stigma and promoting social cohesion.

- Building Resilience: By highlighting successful resolutions and positive changes, transformational narratives contribute to the community's resilience in the face of future conflicts and challenges.

Significance of Transformational Narratives

Transformational narratives hold significant value for individuals, communities, and the broader restorative justice movement.

For Individuals:

1. Healing and Empowerment:

- Victims: Transformational narratives help victims process their trauma, achieve closure, and regain a sense of empowerment.

- Offenders: These stories support offenders in their journey of accountability, remorse, and personal growth, facilitating their rehabilitation and reintegration.

2. Personal Growth:

- Self-Reflection: The process of sharing and listening to transformational narratives encourages self-reflection and personal growth for both victims and offenders.

- Behavioral Change: Understanding the impact of their actions and committing to positive change helps offenders develop pro-social behaviors and reduce the risk of reoffending.

For Communities:

1. Social Cohesion:

- Promoting Understanding: Sharing transformational narratives within the community fosters a culture of empathy, understanding, and mutual respect.

- Reducing Stigma: These stories help reduce the stigma associated with both victimization and offending, promoting a more inclusive and supportive community.

2. Community Resilience:

- Collective Healing: Transformational narratives contribute to collective healing by highlighting successful resolutions and positive outcomes, reinforcing the community's ability to overcome adversity.

- Preventive Measures: By demonstrating the effectiveness of restorative justice, these narratives encourage the adoption of restorative practices as preventive measures for future conflicts.

For the Restorative Justice Movement:

1. Evidence of Success:

- Demonstrating Impact: Transformational narratives provide tangible evidence of the success and impact of restorative justice, supporting its broader implementation and acceptance.

- Building Support: Sharing these stories helps build support for restorative justice among policymakers, practitioners, and the public.

2. Guiding Best Practices:

- Learning from Experience: Analyzing transformational narratives helps identify best practices and areas for improvement, guiding the ongoing development and refinement of restorative justice processes.

- Inspiring Innovation: These stories inspire innovation in restorative justice, encouraging the development of new approaches and techniques to enhance its effectiveness.

Case Studies of Transformational Narratives

Real-life case studies illustrate the power of transformational narratives in fostering healing, understanding, and positive change.

Case Study 1: Overcoming Fear and Building Trust

Background:

- A woman named Lisa was assaulted by a neighbor, which left her with deep emotional scars and a profound fear of her community.

Mediation Process:

- Storytelling: During mediation, Lisa shared her experience and the lasting impact of the assault. Her neighbor,

John, expressed deep remorse and explained the circumstances that led to his actions.

- Active Listening: Both parties engaged in active listening, allowing them to understand each other's perspectives.

- Reparation Agreement: John agreed to participate in anger management counseling and community service as part of the reparation agreement.

Outcome:

- Healing: Lisa found emotional release and began to rebuild her sense of safety and trust in her community.

- Personal Growth: John experienced a significant shift in perspective, committed to personal growth, and worked to make amends.

- Community Impact: The story of Lisa and John's reconciliation was shared within the community, fostering a sense of collective healing and resilience.

Case Study 2: Reconciliation After Tragic Loss
Background:

- A young man named Michael was involved in a car accident that resulted in the death of a teenager, Emily. The incident devastated Emily's family and created a deep rift in the community.

Mediation Process:

- Storytelling: Emily's parents shared their grief and the profound impact of their loss. Michael expressed his remorse and the weight of his guilt.

- Empathy-Building Exercises: Mediators facilitated exercises to help both parties understand each other's pain and perspective.

- Restitution Plan: Michael agreed to speak at local schools about the dangers of reckless driving and to participate in a scholarship fund in Emily's name.

Outcome:

- Healing: Emily's parents found some measure of closure and a way to honor their daughter's memory positively.

- Personal Growth: Michael's involvement in community service and the scholarship fund helped him channel his remorse into positive actions.

- Community Impact: The community witnessed the power of reconciliation and the positive outcomes of restorative justice, reinforcing the value of empathy and understanding.

Promoting Transformational Narratives

To maximize the impact of transformational narratives, it is essential to promote and share these stories within and beyond the community.

Strategies for Promoting Transformational Narratives:

1. Community Forums:

- Public Sharing: Organize community forums where individuals can share their transformational narratives, fostering a culture of openness and understanding.

- Panel Discussions: Host panel discussions with victims, offenders, mediators, and community leaders to discuss the impact of restorative justice and share insights.

2. Media and Publications:

- Storytelling Campaigns: Launch storytelling campaigns in local media, highlighting transformational narratives and the benefits of restorative justice.

- Published Case Studies: Publish detailed case studies in academic journals, books, and online platforms to reach a broader audience and contribute to the evidence base.

3. Educational Programs:

- Restorative Justice Education: Incorporate transformational narratives into restorative justice education programs for schools, universities, and professional training.

- Workshops and Seminars: Conduct workshops and seminars that focus on the power of storytelling and the impact of restorative justice, using real-life examples to illustrate key concepts.

4. Support Networks:

- Peer Support Groups: Establish peer support groups where individuals can share their experiences and learn from each other's transformational narratives.

- Mentorship Programs: Create mentorship programs that pair individuals who have successfully navigated the restorative justice process with those currently going through it, providing guidance and support.

Conclusion

Transformational narratives are powerful stories that emerge from the victim-offender mediation process, illustrating the journey from harm to healing for individuals and communities. These narratives showcase the potential for positive change and highlight the impact of restorative justice in fostering resilience and reconciliation. By promoting empathy, understanding, and personal growth, transformational narratives contribute to collective healing, social cohesion, and a more compassionate community. As restorative justice practices continue to evolve, the lessons learned from these narratives will play a crucial role in guiding future efforts and enhancing the effectiveness of mediation processes. Sharing and celebrating transformational narratives helps build support for restorative justice and inspires ongoing innovation and improvement, ultimately contributing to a more just and empathetic society.

145

CHAPTER 07

LEGAL AND POLICY FRAMEWORKS

Integrating Mediation into Legal Systems

Integrating victim-offender mediation into legal systems is essential for ensuring that restorative justice practices are effectively utilized and supported within the broader framework of criminal justice. This integration requires the development of supportive legal and policy frameworks, the creation of pathways for mediation within the justice system, the establishment of standards and protocols, and the legal recognition of agreements reached through mediation. This chapter explores the steps and considerations involved in integrating mediation into legal systems, highlighting best practices and challenges.

Creating Pathways for Mediation

To successfully integrate victim-offender mediation into legal systems, it is crucial to create clear pathways for mediation at various stages of the justice process. These pathways ensure that mediation is accessible and can be appropriately utilized as an alternative or complement to traditional legal proceedings.

Pre-Charge Mediation:

1. Early Intervention: Pre-charge mediation involves diverting cases to mediation before formal charges are filed. This early intervention can prevent further escalation and promote swift resolution.

2. Criteria for Eligibility: Establishing clear criteria for which cases are eligible for pre-charge mediation helps ensure that the process is applied consistently and appropriately.

Post-Charge but Pre-Trial Mediation:

1. Adjournment for Mediation: In cases where charges have been filed, courts can adjourn proceedings to allow for mediation. This approach provides an opportunity for resolution without proceeding to trial.

2. Judicial Support: Judicial support and encouragement for mediation can facilitate its use and integration within the pre-trial phase.

Post-Conviction Mediation:

1. Rehabilitative Focus: Post-conviction mediation can be used as part of the sentencing or rehabilitative process, focusing on accountability, restitution, and reintegration.

2. Restorative Sentencing Options: Courts can incorporate restorative sentencing options that include mediation as a component of the offender's rehabilitation plan.

Post-Sentencing Mediation:

1. Reintegration Support: Post-sentencing mediation can support the reintegration of offenders into the community, addressing ongoing conflicts and promoting healing.

2. Community-Based Programs: Establishing community-based mediation programs can provide ongoing support and opportunities for restorative justice beyond the formal justice system.

Establishing Standards and Protocols

To ensure the effectiveness and integrity of victim-offender mediation, it is essential to establish clear standards and protocols. These guidelines help maintain consistency, fairness, and accountability within the mediation process.

Standards for Mediators:

1. Qualifications and Training: Establishing minimum qualifications and training requirements for mediators ensures

that they possess the necessary skills and knowledge to facilitate mediation effectively.

2. Certification and Accreditation: Implementing certification and accreditation programs for mediators helps maintain high standards of practice and professionalism.

Protocols for Mediation:

1. Referral Procedures: Developing standardized referral procedures helps ensure that cases are referred to mediation appropriately and efficiently. This includes criteria for eligibility and protocols for judicial referrals.

2. Informed Consent: Ensuring that participants provide informed consent is crucial. Protocols should include clear guidelines for explaining the mediation process, its benefits, and potential outcomes to participants.

Confidentiality and Privacy:

1. Confidentiality Agreements: Establishing confidentiality agreements helps protect the privacy of participants and the integrity of the mediation process.

2. Exceptions to Confidentiality: Clearly outlining exceptions to confidentiality, such as mandatory reporting requirements, helps manage participant expectations and legal obligations.

Monitoring and Evaluation:

1. Quality Assurance: Implementing quality assurance measures, such as regular monitoring and evaluation of mediation programs, helps maintain high standards and identify areas for improvement.

2. Feedback Mechanisms: Creating mechanisms for participant feedback allows for continuous improvement and responsiveness to the needs of those involved in mediation.

Legal Recognition of Mediation Agreements

For mediation to be fully integrated into legal systems, it is essential that agreements reached through mediation are legally recognized and enforceable. This legal recognition provides credibility and ensures that the outcomes of mediation are respected and implemented.

Enforceability of Agreements:

1. Legal Binding: Ensuring that mediation agreements are legally binding and enforceable helps secure the commitment of participants to the terms of the agreement.

2. Judicial Approval: Providing mechanisms for judicial approval of mediation agreements can enhance their enforceability and integration within the formal justice system.

Incorporation into Sentencing:

1. Restorative Sentencing Options: Incorporating mediation agreements into sentencing options allows for

restorative justice principles to be applied within the formal sentencing process.

2. Conditional Sentences: Courts can use conditional sentences that incorporate mediation agreements, providing a structured and enforceable framework for restitution and rehabilitation.

Supportive Legislation:

1. Restorative Justice Legislation: Enacting restorative justice legislation that explicitly supports and integrates mediation into the justice system provides a strong legal foundation for its use.

2. Policy Frameworks: Developing comprehensive policy frameworks that outline the roles, responsibilities, and procedures for mediation helps ensure consistent application and support.

Best Practices for Integration

Integrating victim-offender mediation into legal systems requires careful planning, collaboration, and commitment. Best practices for successful integration include:

Collaboration and Partnership:

1. Stakeholder Engagement: Engaging stakeholders, including the judiciary, law enforcement, legal professionals,

and community organizations, fosters collaboration and support for mediation.

2. Interagency Coordination: Establishing interagency coordination mechanisms helps streamline referral processes and ensure that mediation is integrated smoothly into the justice system.

Education and Training:

1. Judicial Training: Providing training for judges and court personnel on the benefits and processes of mediation helps build support and understanding within the judiciary.

2. Public Awareness: Promoting public awareness of mediation and its benefits helps encourage its use and acceptance within the community.

Resource Allocation:

1. Funding and Support: Ensuring adequate funding and support for mediation programs is essential for their sustainability and effectiveness.

2. Infrastructure Development: Developing the necessary infrastructure, such as mediation centers and support services, helps facilitate the integration of mediation into the justice system.

Continuous Improvement:

1. Evaluation and Research: Conducting ongoing evaluation and research on mediation programs helps identify

best practices, measure impact, and inform policy development.

2. Innovation and Adaptation: Encouraging innovation and adaptation of mediation practices to meet the evolving needs of the justice system and community ensures continued relevance and effectiveness.

Challenges and Considerations

While integrating victim-offender mediation into legal systems offers numerous benefits, it also presents challenges that must be addressed.

Resistance to Change:

1. Institutional Resistance: Resistance to change within the legal system can hinder the integration of mediation. Building awareness and demonstrating the benefits of mediation can help overcome this resistance.

2. Cultural Barriers: Cultural barriers and misconceptions about mediation may affect its acceptance. Education and outreach efforts are essential to address these barriers.

Resource Constraints:

1. Funding Limitations: Limited funding and resources can impact the availability and quality of mediation programs. Advocating for increased funding and support is crucial.

2. Access and Availability: Ensuring that mediation is accessible to all participants, regardless of geographic location or socioeconomic status, is essential for equitable implementation.

Maintaining Quality and Consistency:

1. Standardization: Balancing the need for standardized protocols with the flexibility to address individual case needs can be challenging. Developing clear guidelines and best practices helps maintain consistency and quality.

2. Mediator Competence: Ensuring that mediators maintain high levels of competence and professionalism through ongoing training and certification is essential for effective mediation.

Conclusion

Integrating victim-offender mediation into legal systems requires the development of supportive legal and policy frameworks, the creation of clear pathways for mediation within the justice system, the establishment of standards and protocols, and the legal recognition of mediation agreements. By following best practices, addressing challenges, and fostering collaboration among stakeholders, mediation can be effectively integrated into the justice system, offering a restorative and transformative approach to resolving conflicts and promoting healing. As restorative justice practices continue to evolve, the integration of mediation into legal systems will play a crucial role in enhancing the effectiveness and reach of these practices, ultimately contributing to a more just and compassionate society.

Policy Development and Support

The sustainability and expansion of restorative justice practices, including victim-offender mediation, rely heavily on comprehensive policy development and robust institutional support. Governments and institutions must invest in training, resources, and infrastructure to ensure that mediation programs are effective and accessible. This chapter explores the essential components of policy development and support, highlighting the role of government, institutional commitment, and the necessary investments to foster the growth and success of restorative justice initiatives.

The Role of Government in Policy Development

Governments play a pivotal role in developing policies that support restorative justice practices. Effective policy development involves creating a legal and regulatory framework that promotes the use of mediation and other restorative practices within the justice system.

Legislative Framework:

1. Restorative Justice Legislation: Enacting specific legislation that supports and mandates the use of restorative justice practices, including victim-offender mediation, provides a solid legal foundation for these programs.

2. Integration with Existing Laws: Ensuring that restorative justice policies are integrated with existing criminal justice laws and procedures helps create a cohesive and comprehensive legal framework.

Funding and Resources:

1. Budget Allocations: Allocating sufficient budgetary resources for the development and implementation of restorative justice programs is crucial for their sustainability.

2. Grant Programs: Establishing grant programs to support community-based organizations and initiatives that promote restorative justice can enhance the reach and impact of these practices.

Oversight and Evaluation:

1. Monitoring and Accountability: Creating oversight bodies or committees to monitor the implementation and effectiveness of restorative justice programs ensures accountability and continuous improvement.

2. Data Collection and Research: Investing in data collection and research to evaluate the outcomes and impact

of restorative justice practices provides evidence to support ongoing policy development and refinement.

Institutional Commitment and Support

Institutions, including the judiciary, law enforcement agencies, educational institutions, and community organizations, must demonstrate a strong commitment to restorative justice principles and practices. This commitment is essential for the successful implementation and expansion of mediation programs.

Judicial Support:

1. Judicial Training: Providing training for judges and court personnel on the principles and benefits of restorative justice helps build support within the judiciary.

2. Restorative Sentencing Options: Encouraging judges to incorporate restorative sentencing options, such as victim-offender mediation, into their judicial decisions promotes the use of restorative justice within the court system.

Law Enforcement Engagement:

1. Police Training: Training police officers on restorative justice practices and the benefits of victim-offender mediation fosters a collaborative approach to conflict resolution.

2. Referral Programs: Establishing referral programs that allow law enforcement to refer appropriate cases to mediation can enhance the use of restorative practices within the justice system.

Educational Institutions:

1. Restorative Justice Education: Incorporating restorative justice principles into educational curricula at all levels helps raise awareness and build a culture of restorative practices from a young age.

2. School-Based Programs: Developing school-based mediation programs can address conflicts within educational settings and promote a restorative approach to discipline.

Community Organizations:

1. Community Partnerships: Building partnerships with community organizations that provide mediation services helps expand the reach of restorative justice programs and ensures that they are accessible to diverse populations.

2. Capacity Building: Investing in the capacity building of community organizations through training and funding support strengthens their ability to deliver effective mediation services.

Investments in Training and Professional Development

Investing in the training and professional development of mediators and other restorative justice practitioners is essential for maintaining high standards of practice and ensuring the effectiveness of mediation programs.

Training Programs:

1. Initial Training: Comprehensive initial training programs that cover the principles of restorative justice, mediation techniques, and conflict resolution skills are crucial for preparing new mediators.

2. Specialized Training: Offering specialized training in areas such as trauma-informed practice, cultural competency, and dealing with specific types of conflicts enhances the skills and effectiveness of mediators.

Continuous Professional Development:

1. Ongoing Education: Providing opportunities for ongoing education and professional development helps mediators stay current with the latest research, techniques, and best practices in restorative justice.

2. Certification and Accreditation: Implementing certification and accreditation programs for mediators ensures that they meet established standards of practice and professionalism.

Supervision and Mentorship:

1. Supervision Programs: Establishing supervision programs where experienced mediators provide guidance and support to less experienced practitioners helps maintain quality and effectiveness.

2. Mentorship Opportunities: Creating mentorship opportunities where seasoned mediators mentor new practitioners fosters a culture of continuous learning and professional growth.

Building Infrastructure for Mediation Programs

Developing the necessary infrastructure to support mediation programs is critical for their accessibility and sustainability. This includes creating physical spaces for mediation, establishing administrative support systems, and leveraging technology.

Physical Spaces:

1. Mediation Centers: Establishing dedicated mediation centers that provide safe and neutral environments for mediation sessions ensures that these services are accessible and professional.

2. Community-Based Locations: Utilizing community-based locations such as schools, community centers, and religious institutions for mediation sessions can enhance accessibility and comfort for participants.

Administrative Support:

1. Program Management: Developing robust program management structures that include administrative support, case management, and logistical coordination is essential for the smooth operation of mediation programs.

2. Resource Allocation: Allocating resources for administrative functions such as scheduling, record-keeping, and participant support ensures the efficiency and effectiveness of mediation programs.

Leveraging Technology:

1. Online Mediation Platforms: Utilizing online mediation platforms can expand access to mediation services, particularly for individuals in remote or underserved areas.

2. Digital Case Management: Implementing digital case management systems helps streamline administrative processes and improve data collection and analysis.

Promoting Public Awareness and Engagement

Raising public awareness and fostering engagement with restorative justice practices are crucial for building support and ensuring the success of mediation programs.

Public Education Campaigns:

1. Awareness Campaigns: Launching public education campaigns that highlight the benefits and successes of restorative justice and mediation helps build community support and encourage participation.

2. Media Outreach: Utilizing media outlets, including social media, to share stories and testimonials from participants can raise awareness and promote the positive impact of restorative justice.

Community Involvement:

1. Community Forums: Organizing community forums and town hall meetings to discuss restorative justice practices and gather input from community members fosters engagement and collaboration.

2. Stakeholder Collaboration: Engaging stakeholders, including victims, offenders, community leaders, and service providers, in the development and implementation of mediation programs ensures that these initiatives are responsive to community needs.

Policy Advocacy:

1. Advocacy Groups: Supporting advocacy groups that promote restorative justice and mediation helps influence policy development and secure funding and resources.

2. Legislative Support: Working with legislators to develop and pass supportive policies and legislation ensures that restorative justice practices are recognized and integrated into the formal justice system.

Conclusion

Policy development and support are critical for the sustainability and expansion of restorative justice practices, including victim-offender mediation. Governments and institutions must invest in training, resources, and infrastructure to ensure the effectiveness and accessibility of mediation programs. By creating supportive legal frameworks, fostering institutional commitment, investing in professional development, building necessary infrastructure, and promoting public awareness, policymakers can enhance the impact and reach of restorative justice. These efforts will contribute to a more just and compassionate society, where conflicts are resolved through healing and reconciliation, rather than punishment and retribution.

International Perspectives

Restorative justice practices, including victim-offender mediation, vary significantly across different legal and cultural contexts. Examining international perspectives provides valuable insights into how these practices can be adapted and implemented in diverse settings. This chapter explores restorative justice models from various countries, highlighting best practices, cultural adaptations, and the challenges faced in different legal systems. By understanding these international perspectives, policymakers and practitioners can develop more effective and culturally sensitive restorative justice programs.

Restorative Justice Models from Around the World

Several countries have successfully integrated restorative justice practices into their legal systems, each with unique approaches and adaptations. The following case studies illustrate how victim-offender mediation and other restorative practices are implemented in various international contexts.

New Zealand: The Family Group Conference Model

Background:

- New Zealand is renowned for its pioneering use of restorative justice, particularly through the Family Group Conference (FGC) model, which was established under the Children, Young Persons, and Their Families Act 1989.

Key Features:

- Involvement of Family and Community: FGCs involve not only the victim and offender but also their families, community members, and other relevant parties. This holistic approach ensures that the needs of all stakeholders are addressed.

- Cultural Sensitivity: The model is deeply rooted in the Maori tradition of collective decision-making, emphasizing cultural sensitivity and community involvement.

- Focus on Youth Justice: FGCs are primarily used in the youth justice system, providing a supportive environment for young offenders to take responsibility and make amends.

Outcomes:

- Reduction in Reoffending: Studies have shown that FGCs contribute to lower recidivism rates among young offenders.

- Community Empowerment: The model empowers communities to take an active role in the justice process, promoting social cohesion and collective responsibility.

Canada: Restorative Justice Circles

Background:

- Canada has a rich history of restorative justice practices, with significant contributions from Indigenous communities and their traditional conflict resolution methods.

Key Features:

- Circle Process: Restorative justice circles involve participants sitting in a circle, symbolizing equality and inclusiveness. The process is guided by a facilitator or "circle keeper."

- Indigenous Traditions: The circle process is inspired by Indigenous practices, emphasizing healing, respect, and the interconnectedness of all community members.

- Application in Various Contexts: Circles are used in a wide range of contexts, including criminal justice, schools, workplaces, and community disputes.

Outcomes:

- Healing and Reconciliation: Circles provide a safe space for participants to share their stories, express emotions, and work towards healing and reconciliation.

- Cultural Integration: The use of circles honors Indigenous traditions and promotes cultural sensitivity and respect.

Norway: Mediation and Reconciliation Services

Background:

- Norway has integrated restorative justice into its legal system through the Mediation and Reconciliation Service (Konfliktrådet), established in 1991.

Key Features:

- Voluntary Participation: Participation in mediation is voluntary for both victims and offenders, ensuring that all parties engage willingly.

- Trained Mediators: The service employs trained mediators who facilitate dialogue and help parties reach mutually acceptable agreements.

- Nationwide Availability: Mediation and reconciliation services are available across the country, making restorative justice accessible to a broad population.

Outcomes:

- High Satisfaction Rates: Surveys indicate high levels of satisfaction among participants, with many reporting that mediation helped them feel heard and respected.

- Integration with Legal System: The service is well-integrated into the Norwegian legal system, offering an alternative to traditional criminal proceedings.

South Africa: Ubuntu and Restorative Justice

Background:

- South Africa's approach to restorative justice is influenced by the concept of Ubuntu, which emphasizes human interconnectedness, compassion, and community.

Key Features:

- Community-Based Practices: Restorative justice practices are often community-based, involving local leaders and community members in the process.

- Focus on Reconciliation: Given South Africa's history of apartheid, restorative justice focuses on reconciliation and rebuilding relationships within communities.

- Integration with Formal Justice: Restorative practices are integrated with the formal justice system, providing complementary approaches to conflict resolution.

Outcomes:

- Promotion of Social Harmony: The emphasis on reconciliation and community involvement promotes social harmony and reduces the likelihood of future conflicts.

- Restoration of Relationships: Restorative justice practices help restore relationships damaged by crime and historical injustices.

Adapting Restorative Justice to Cultural Contexts

Cultural context plays a crucial role in the implementation and effectiveness of restorative justice practices. Adapting these practices to align with cultural values, traditions, and social norms is essential for their success.

Understanding Cultural Values:

1. Respect for Traditions: Incorporating local traditions and cultural practices into restorative justice models ensures that they resonate with participants and are culturally appropriate.

2. Community Involvement: Engaging community leaders and members in the development and implementation

of restorative justice programs fosters acceptance and support.

Addressing Cultural Sensitivities:

1. Language and Communication: Using language and communication styles that are culturally sensitive helps build trust and facilitate effective dialogue.

2. Training for Mediators: Providing cultural competency training for mediators ensures that they are aware of and can navigate cultural nuances during the mediation process.

Incorporating Indigenous Practices:

1. Learning from Indigenous Methods: Many Indigenous communities have long-standing traditions of restorative justice. Integrating these methods into broader restorative justice programs can enhance their effectiveness and cultural relevance.

2. Respecting Indigenous Sovereignty: Ensuring that Indigenous communities have autonomy and leadership in developing and implementing restorative justice practices respects their sovereignty and promotes self-determination.

Challenges and Opportunities in International Contexts

While restorative justice offers numerous benefits, its implementation in diverse international contexts presents challenges that must be addressed.

Challenges:

1. Legal Barriers: Differences in legal systems and regulations can hinder the integration of restorative justice practices. Adapting these practices to align with local laws and policies is essential.

2. Resource Constraints: Limited resources and funding can impact the availability and quality of restorative justice programs. Securing adequate funding and support is crucial for sustainability.

3. Resistance to Change: Resistance from traditional justice institutions and stakeholders can impede the adoption of restorative justice practices. Building awareness and demonstrating the benefits of these practices can help overcome resistance.

Opportunities:

1. Global Learning and Exchange: Sharing knowledge and experiences across countries can foster innovation and improvement in restorative justice practices. International conferences, networks, and collaborations provide platforms for this exchange.

2. Policy Advocacy: Advocating for supportive policies and legislation at the national and international levels can enhance the integration and recognition of restorative justice practices.

3. Technological Advancements: Leveraging technology, such as online mediation platforms, can expand access to restorative justice services, particularly in remote or underserved areas.

Best Practices for Implementing Restorative Justice Internationally

Based on international experiences, several best practices have emerged for implementing restorative justice effectively in diverse cultural and legal contexts.

Engage Stakeholders:

1. Inclusive Planning: Involve a wide range of stakeholders, including victims, offenders, community members, legal professionals, and policymakers, in the planning and implementation of restorative justice programs.

2. Community Partnerships: Build strong partnerships with community organizations, Indigenous groups, and local leaders to ensure that programs are culturally relevant and supported.

Develop Comprehensive Policies:

1. Supportive Legislation: Advocate for and develop legislation that explicitly supports restorative justice practices and provides a legal framework for their implementation.

2. Clear Protocols: Establish clear protocols and guidelines for the referral, implementation, and evaluation of restorative justice programs to ensure consistency and effectiveness.

Invest in Training and Capacity Building:

1. Mediator Training: Provide comprehensive training for mediators, including cultural competency, trauma-informed practice, and conflict resolution skills.

2. Professional Development: Offer ongoing professional development opportunities for practitioners to stay current with best practices and innovations in restorative justice.

Promote Public Awareness:

1. Education Campaigns: Launch public education campaigns to raise awareness about the benefits and principles of restorative justice.

2. Media Engagement: Utilize media outlets to share success stories and testimonials, highlighting the positive impact of restorative justice on individuals and communities.

Conclusion

Examining international perspectives on restorative justice provides valuable insights into how victim-offender mediation and other restorative practices can be adapted and implemented in diverse cultural and legal contexts. By understanding the unique approaches and challenges faced by different countries, policymakers and practitioners can develop more effective and culturally sensitive restorative justice programs. Engaging stakeholders, developing comprehensive policies, investing in training and capacity building, and promoting public awareness are critical steps for successfully integrating restorative justice practices worldwide. These efforts will contribute to a more just and compassionate global society, where conflicts are resolved through healing and reconciliation rather than punishment and retribution.

CHAPTER 08

CULTURAL SENSITIVITY IN MEDIATION

Respecting Diversity and Inclusion

Cultural sensitivity is essential in victim-offender mediation to ensure the process is accessible, respectful, and meaningful for participants from diverse backgrounds. Mediators must be aware of and respect cultural norms, values, and communication styles to effectively facilitate the mediation process. This chapter explores the importance of cultural sensitivity, strategies for respecting diversity and inclusion, and the role of mediators in creating a culturally responsive mediation environment.

The Importance of Cultural Sensitivity

Cultural sensitivity in mediation is vital for several reasons:

1. Building Trust and Rapport:

- Respecting Cultural Norms: Acknowledging and respecting cultural norms and values helps build trust and rapport between mediators and participants.

- Enhancing Communication: Understanding cultural differences in communication styles ensures that all participants feel heard and respected.

2. Ensuring Fairness and Equity:

- Addressing Power Imbalances: Being aware of cultural dynamics helps mediators address power imbalances and ensure that all participants have an equal voice.

- Promoting Inclusion: Cultural sensitivity promotes inclusion, ensuring that mediation is accessible and relevant to participants from diverse backgrounds.

3. Facilitating Healing and Reconciliation:

- Acknowledging Cultural Trauma: Recognizing the impact of cultural trauma and historical injustices helps create a supportive environment for healing and reconciliation.

- Respecting Cultural Practices: Incorporating cultural practices and traditions into the mediation process can enhance its effectiveness and relevance.

Strategies for Respecting Diversity and Inclusion

Mediators can employ several strategies to respect diversity and inclusion in the mediation process:

1. Cultural Competency Training:

- Continuous Learning: Mediators should engage in continuous learning about different cultures, including their norms, values, and communication styles.

- Specialized Training: Participating in specialized cultural competency training helps mediators develop the skills needed to navigate cultural differences effectively.

2. Inclusive Communication:

- Language Access: Providing interpretation and translation services ensures that participants who speak different languages can fully engage in the mediation process.

- Culturally Appropriate Language: Using language that is culturally appropriate and sensitive helps avoid misunderstandings and shows respect for participants' backgrounds.

3. Creating a Culturally Responsive Environment:

- Physical Space: Designing mediation spaces that are welcoming and reflective of participants' cultures can help create a sense of comfort and belonging.

- Cultural Practices: Incorporating cultural practices and rituals into the mediation process, when appropriate, shows respect for participants' traditions and enhances the process's relevance.

4. Engaging Community Resources:

- Community Leaders: Involving community leaders and cultural representatives in the mediation process can provide valuable insights and support for participants.

- Cultural Organizations: Partnering with cultural organizations helps mediators access resources and expertise that can enhance the mediation process.

The Role of Mediators in Creating a Culturally Responsive Environment

Mediators play a crucial role in ensuring that the mediation process respects diversity and inclusion. They must be proactive in creating a culturally responsive environment and addressing the needs of participants from diverse backgrounds.

1. Building Cultural Awareness:

- Self-Reflection: Mediators should engage in self-reflection to recognize their own cultural biases and assumptions and understand how these may impact their mediation practice.

- Cultural Knowledge: Gaining knowledge about the cultural backgrounds of participants helps mediators understand their perspectives and needs.

2. Facilitating Inclusive Dialogue:

- Encouraging Participation: Mediators should encourage all participants to share their perspectives and experiences, ensuring that diverse voices are heard.

- Respecting Differences: Acknowledging and respecting differences in communication styles, decision-making processes, and conflict resolution approaches is essential for effective mediation.

3. Addressing Cultural Conflicts:

- Identifying Cultural Issues: Mediators should be skilled in identifying cultural issues that may arise during mediation and addressing them constructively.

- Cultural Adaptation: Adapting mediation techniques to align with participants' cultural values and norms can enhance the process's effectiveness and relevance.

4. Ensuring Accessibility:

- Removing Barriers: Identifying and removing barriers to participation, such as language, transportation, and financial constraints, ensures that mediation is accessible to all participants.

- Providing Support: Offering support services, such as childcare, transportation assistance, and emotional support, help participants engage fully in the mediation process.

Case Studies: Culturally Sensitive Mediation

The following case studies illustrate the importance of cultural sensitivity in mediation and highlight effective strategies for respecting diversity and inclusion.

Case Study 1: Mediating in a Multicultural Community

Background:

- A conflict arose between two families from different cultural backgrounds in a multicultural community. The dispute involved property boundaries and was exacerbated by cultural misunderstandings.

Mediation Process:

- Cultural Competency: The mediator, trained in cultural competency, took time to learn about the cultural backgrounds of both families and the cultural significance of property in their respective traditions.

- Inclusive Communication: Interpretation services were provided to ensure that language barriers did not hinder communication. The mediator used culturally appropriate language to facilitate dialogue.

- Engaging Community Leaders: Community leaders from both cultural groups were invited to participate in the mediation, providing cultural insights and supporting the process.

Outcome:

- Resolution: The families reached an agreement that respected their cultural values and addressed the property dispute. The involvement of community leaders helped build trust and ensure the agreement's acceptance.

- Healing: The mediation process helped repair relationships and promote understanding between the families, fostering a sense of community cohesion.

Case Study 2: Incorporating Indigenous Practices in Mediation

Background:

- A young Indigenous offender was involved in a vandalism incident that affected a local business. The business owner, also Indigenous, sought a restorative justice approach.

Mediation Process:

- Cultural Practices: The mediator incorporated Indigenous practices, such as a traditional talking circle, into the mediation process. This approach respected the cultural heritage of both parties and provided a familiar and comfortable setting for dialogue.

- Community Involvement: Elders and community members were invited to participate, offering guidance and support to both the victim and the offender.

- Respecting Traditions: The mediation process included traditional prayers and ceremonies, which honored the cultural traditions of the participants.

Outcome:

- Resolution: The offender took responsibility for the vandalism and agreed to make amends by participating in community service and cultural education programs. The business owner felt heard and respected, leading to a sense of closure and healing.

- Community Impact: The mediation process strengthened community ties and highlighted the importance of integrating cultural practices into restorative justice approaches.

Challenges and Considerations in Culturally Sensitive Mediation

While cultural sensitivity is essential for effective mediation, it also presents challenges that mediators must navigate.

Challenges:

- Cultural Misunderstandings: Misunderstandings and miscommunications can arise from cultural differences, potentially hindering the mediation process.

- Balancing Cultural Sensitivity and Legal Requirements: Mediators must balance respecting cultural practices with adhering to legal requirements and standards.

- Power Dynamics: Cultural differences can exacerbate power imbalances, requiring mediators to be particularly attentive to ensuring equity and fairness.

Considerations:

- Continuous Learning: Mediators must commit to continuous learning and self-improvement to enhance their cultural competency and effectiveness.

- Flexibility: Being flexible and adaptable in mediation techniques allows mediators to respond to the unique cultural needs of participants.

- Collaboration: Collaborating with cultural experts, community leaders, and organizations can provide valuable support and resources for culturally sensitive mediation.

Conclusion

Respecting diversity and inclusion is crucial for the success of victim-offender mediation. Cultural sensitivity ensures that the mediation process is accessible, respectful, and meaningful for participants from diverse backgrounds. Mediators play a vital role in creating a culturally responsive environment by building cultural awareness, facilitating inclusive dialogue, addressing cultural conflicts, and ensuring accessibility. By employing strategies such as cultural competency training, inclusive communication, and community engagement, mediators can enhance the effectiveness of restorative justice practices and promote healing and reconciliation in diverse cultural contexts. The commitment to cultural sensitivity and inclusion not only strengthens the mediation process but also contributes to a more just and equitable society.

Adapting Practices to Different Cultures

Adapting mediation practices to different cultures involves flexibility, creativity, and a deep understanding of the cultural context in which mediation occurs. This adaptation may include using culturally relevant symbols, rituals, and languages to facilitate dialogue and ensure participants feel comfortable and respected. By tailoring mediation practices to the cultural backgrounds of participants, mediators can enhance the effectiveness and inclusiveness of the restorative justice process. This chapter explores strategies for adapting mediation practices to different cultures, the importance of cultural relevance, and practical examples of successful adaptations.

The Importance of Cultural Relevance in Mediation

Cultural relevance in mediation is essential for several reasons:

1. Building Trust and Rapport:

- Respect for Cultural Norms: Demonstrating respect for participants' cultural norms and values helps build trust and rapport, which are crucial for effective mediation.

- Enhancing Engagement: When participants see their cultural practices and symbols reflected in the mediation process, they are more likely to engage meaningfully and openly.

2. Ensuring Effective Communication:

- Language and Expression: Using participants' native languages and culturally appropriate expressions ensures clear communication and reduces misunderstandings.

- Non-Verbal Cues: Being aware of and respecting cultural differences in non-verbal communication, such as gestures and body language, enhances understanding.

3. Facilitating Emotional and Psychological Comfort:

- Familiar Practices: Incorporating familiar cultural practices and rituals creates a sense of comfort and safety for participants.

- Respecting Cultural Identities: Acknowledging and honoring participants' cultural identities helps them feel respected and valued.

Strategies for Adapting Mediation Practices

Mediators can employ various strategies to adapt mediation practices to different cultural contexts effectively:

1. Conducting Cultural Research:

- Understanding Cultural Backgrounds: Conducting research on the cultural backgrounds of participants helps mediators understand their values, beliefs, and practices.

- Consulting Cultural Experts: Engaging with cultural experts and community leaders provides valuable insights and guidance on cultural nuances.

2. Using Culturally Relevant Symbols and Rituals:

- Incorporating Symbols: Using culturally relevant symbols in the mediation setting, such as artwork, artifacts, or decorations, creates a welcoming environment.

- Adapting Rituals: Integrating cultural rituals and ceremonies, such as traditional prayers, blessings, or greetings, into the mediation process respects participants' traditions and enhances their comfort.

3. Providing Language Support:

- Translation and Interpretation Services: Offering translation and interpretation services ensures that language barriers do not hinder communication and participation.

- Bilingual Mediators: Utilizing bilingual mediators who speak the participants' native languages facilitates clearer communication and understanding.

4. Adapting Communication Styles:

- Verbal Communication: Adapting verbal communication styles to align with cultural norms, such as using honorifics, formal language, or specific terms of respect, helps build rapport and respect.

- Non-Verbal Communication: Being mindful of cultural differences in non-verbal communication, such as eye contact, gestures, and physical proximity, ensures respectful interactions.

5. Creating a Culturally Inclusive Environment:

- Physical Setting: Designing the physical setting of the mediation space to reflect the cultural backgrounds of participants, such as arranging seating in culturally appropriate ways, enhances comfort and inclusivity.

- Cultural Sensitivity Training: Providing cultural sensitivity training for mediators ensures they are equipped to navigate cultural differences and adapt practices appropriately.

Practical Examples of Culturally Adapted Mediation Practices

The following examples illustrate how mediation practices have been successfully adapted to different cultural contexts:

Example 1: Incorporating Maori Practices in New Zealand

Background:

- In New Zealand, the Family Group Conference (FGC) model incorporates Maori cultural practices to address conflicts and promote healing.

Adaptations:

- Traditional Greetings: The FGC process begins with a traditional Maori greeting (mihi), which sets a respectful tone and honors the cultural heritage of participants.

- Whanau Involvement: The involvement of the extended family (whanau) reflects Maori values of collective responsibility and community support.

- Cultural Symbols: The use of Maori symbols and artifacts in the mediation setting creates a culturally relevant and welcoming environment.

Outcome:

- Enhanced Engagement: Participants engage more meaningfully in the FGC process due to the incorporation of familiar cultural practices.

- Cultural Relevance: The adaptations ensure that the mediation process resonates with Maori participants and respects their cultural identity.

Example 2: Utilizing Restorative Circles in Indigenous Canadian Communities

Background:

- Restorative justice circles, inspired by Indigenous traditions, are widely used in Canadian Indigenous communities to address conflicts and promote healing.

Adaptations:

- Circle Process: Participants sit in a circle, symbolizing equality and inclusiveness, which is a traditional practice in many Indigenous cultures.

- Talking Piece: A talking piece, often a culturally significant object, is used to regulate the flow of conversation, ensuring that everyone has an opportunity to speak.

- Ceremonial Elements: The inclusion of ceremonial elements, such as smudging or traditional prayers, honors Indigenous cultural practices and creates a sacred space for dialogue.

Outcome:

- Cultural Resonance: The use of restorative circles and ceremonial elements ensures that the mediation process aligns with Indigenous cultural values and practices.

- Healing and Reconciliation: The adaptations facilitate deep emotional and psychological healing, promoting reconciliation and community cohesion.

Example 3: Adapting Mediation for South Asian Communities

Background:

- In South Asian communities, conflicts are often resolved through the involvement of elders and extended family members.

Adaptations:

- Elder Involvement: Including respected elders and community leaders in the mediation process reflects the cultural value of elder wisdom and authority.

- Family Participation: Encouraging the participation of extended family members ensures that the mediation process addresses the collective needs and concerns of the family.

- Cultural Rituals: Incorporating cultural rituals, such as offering tea or conducting traditional blessings, creates a familiar and respectful environment.

Outcome:

- Respect for Tradition: The involvement of elders and family members respects cultural traditions and enhances the legitimacy of the mediation process.

- Collective Resolution: The adaptations ensure that the resolution addresses the needs of the entire family, promoting harmony and unity.

Challenges and Considerations in Cultural Adaptation

Adapting mediation practices to different cultures presents challenges that mediators must navigate carefully:

Challenges:

- Cultural Misunderstandings: Misunderstandings and misinterpretations can arise from cultural differences, potentially hindering the mediation process.

- Balancing Cultural Sensitivity and Neutrality: Mediators must balance cultural sensitivity with maintaining neutrality and fairness in the mediation process.

- Resource Constraints: Providing language support and cultural adaptations may require additional resources and funding.

Considerations:

- Continuous Learning: Mediators must commit to continuous learning and self-improvement to enhance their cultural competency and effectiveness.

- Flexibility: Being flexible and adaptable in mediation techniques allows mediators to respond to the unique cultural needs of participants.

- Collaboration: Collaborating with cultural experts, community leaders, and organizations provides valuable support and resources for culturally adapted mediation.

Conclusion

Adapting mediation practices to different cultures is essential for ensuring that the process is accessible, respectful, and meaningful for participants from diverse backgrounds. Mediators must employ flexibility, creativity, and a deep understanding of cultural contexts to effectively facilitate the mediation process. By incorporating culturally relevant symbols, rituals, and languages, and by creating a culturally inclusive environment, mediators can enhance the effectiveness and inclusiveness of restorative justice practices. Practical examples from various cultural contexts illustrate the successful adaptation of mediation practices and highlight the importance of cultural relevance in promoting healing and reconciliation. The commitment to cultural sensitivity and adaptation not only strengthens the mediation process but also contributes to a more just and equitable society.

Case Examples from Various Cultures

Case examples from various cultures illustrate how restorative justice practices can be tailored to meet the unique needs of different communities. These examples provide valuable insights into effective strategies for cultural adaptation and highlight the universal principles of restorative justice. By examining these cases, we can understand how to respect and integrate cultural norms, values, and practices into the mediation process, ensuring it is meaningful and effective for all participants.

Case Example 1: Maori Family Group Conferences in New Zealand

Background:

In New Zealand, the Family Group Conference (FGC) model, influenced by Maori cultural practices, is a cornerstone of the youth justice system. This approach integrates traditional Maori concepts of collective decision-making and community involvement.

Case Details:

A 15-year-old Maori boy, Tama, was involved in a burglary. The victim, a local store owner, and Tama's family participated in the FGC.

Adaptations and Strategies:

1. Cultural Greeting: The conference began with a traditional Maori greeting (mihi) to honor the cultural heritage of the participants.

2. Whanau (Extended Family) Involvement: Tama's extended family (whanau) and community members were actively involved, reflecting the Maori value of collective responsibility.

3. Use of Maori Language and Symbols: The FGC included the use of Maori language and cultural symbols, creating a culturally relevant and respectful environment.

Outcome:

- Restitution Agreement: Tama agreed to work at the store to make amends for the damage caused. The agreement also included participation in community service.

- Healing and Reconciliation: The involvement of the whanau and community fostered a sense of collective healing and reconciliation, reinforcing community ties.

Case Example 2: Indigenous Circle Processes in Canada

Background:

In Canada, restorative justice circles are widely used, particularly within Indigenous communities. These circles are based on traditional Indigenous practices of collective decision-making and healing.

Case Details:

An Indigenous teenager, Emily, was involved in a school altercation that resulted in injuries to another student, Jake.

Adaptations and Strategies:

1. Circle Process: The mediation used a circle process, with all participants, including family members, teachers, and

community elders, sitting in a circle to signify equality and inclusion.

2. Talking Piece: A culturally significant object was used as a talking piece, ensuring that everyone had an opportunity to speak without interruption.

3. Ceremonial Elements: The process included traditional prayers and a smudging ceremony to create a sacred space for dialogue and healing.

Outcome:

- Restorative Agreement: Emily apologized and agreed to participate in a cultural education program and community service. Jake and his family accepted the apology and the steps taken towards restitution.

- Community Healing: The process reinforced community values of empathy, respect, and collective healing, contributing to a supportive school environment.

Case Example 3: Ubuntu-Based Mediation in South Africa

Background:

South Africa's approach to restorative justice is deeply influenced by the concept of Ubuntu, which emphasizes interconnectedness, compassion, and community.

Case Details:

A case involved a young man, Sipho, who had committed theft from a neighbor, Mr. Dlamini. The community sought a restorative justice approach to address the issue.

Adaptations and Strategies:

1. Community-Based Mediation: The mediation was held in a community hall, with the participation of local leaders and community members, reflecting the Ubuntu value of collective resolution.

2. Use of Ubuntu Principles: The mediation emphasized Ubuntu principles, focusing on restoring harmony and rebuilding relationships rather than punishment.

3. Cultural Rituals: The process included traditional blessings and the sharing of a communal meal to foster a sense of unity and reconciliation.

Outcome:

- Restitution Agreement: Sipho agreed to work for Mr. Dlamini and participate in a mentorship program led by community elders.

- Reconciliation: The mediation helped restore trust between Sipho and Mr. Dlamini, and reinforced community bonds, promoting social harmony.

Case Example 4: Restorative Justice in Japanese Schools

Background:

In Japan, restorative justice practices have been integrated into school settings to address conflicts and promote a positive learning environment.

Case Details:

A conflict arose between two students, Hiroshi and Yuki, over bullying incidents. The school adopted a restorative justice approach to resolve the issue.

Adaptations and Strategies:

1. Group Conferencing: A group conference was held with the involvement of the students, their parents, teachers, and a trained mediator.

2. Respectful Communication: The mediation emphasized respectful communication, aligning with Japanese cultural norms of politeness and harmony.

3. Cultural Sensitivity: The process included elements of Japanese culture, such as the use of honorifics and the concept of "saving face," to ensure that the students felt respected and understood.

Outcome:

- Resolution Agreement: Hiroshi apologized to Yuki and agreed to participate in an anti-bullying program. Both students also committed to a school project promoting positive behavior.

- Positive School Climate: The mediation process helped improve the school climate, reducing bullying incidents and promoting a culture of respect and empathy.

Case Example 5: South Asian Community Mediation

Background:

In South Asian communities, conflicts are often resolved with the involvement of elders and extended family members, reflecting cultural values of respect and collective decision-making.

Case Details:

A dispute arose between two families over a business transaction. The mediation was conducted with the involvement of community elders.

Adaptations and Strategies:

1. Elder Involvement: Respected elders from both families participated in the mediation, providing guidance and ensuring that cultural values were respected.

2. Cultural Rituals: The mediation included traditional rituals, such as offering tea and conducting prayers, to create a respectful and familiar environment.

3. Family Participation: The extended families of both parties were involved, ensuring that the resolution addressed the collective needs and concerns of the families.

Outcome:

- Settlement Agreement: The families reached a settlement agreement that included compensation and a commitment to future collaboration. The elders facilitated the agreement and ensured its acceptance.

- Strengthened Relationships: The mediation process helped repair relationships between the families and reinforced community values of respect and cooperation.

Challenges and Considerations in Adapting Practices

Adapting mediation practices to different cultural contexts presents challenges that must be navigated carefully:

Challenges:

- Cultural Misunderstandings: Differences in cultural norms and values can lead to misunderstandings and misinterpretations during the mediation process.

- Resource Constraints: Providing language support, cultural adaptations, and training for mediators may require additional resources and funding.

- Balancing Cultural Sensitivity and Legal Requirements: Mediators must balance the need for cultural sensitivity with adherence to legal standards and ethical guidelines.

Considerations:

- Continuous Learning: Mediators must commit to continuous learning and self-improvement to enhance their cultural competency and effectiveness.

- Flexibility: Being flexible and adaptable in mediation techniques allows mediators to respond to the unique cultural needs of participants.

- Collaboration: Collaborating with cultural experts, community leaders, and organizations provides valuable support and resources for culturally adapted mediation.

Conclusion

Case examples from various cultures illustrate how restorative justice practices can be tailored to meet the needs of different communities. These examples demonstrate effective strategies for cultural adaptation, such as incorporating culturally relevant symbols, rituals, and languages, and involving community leaders and elders. By respecting and integrating cultural norms and values, mediators can create a more inclusive, respectful, and effective mediation process. The universal principles of restorative justice, such as empathy, respect, and healing, can be applied across diverse cultural contexts, promoting reconciliation and social harmony. Through continuous learning and collaboration, mediators can enhance their cultural competency and contribute to a more just and equitable society.

CHAPTER 09

TRAINING AND EDUCATION FOR PRACTITIONERS

Curriculum Development

Developing curricula for training restorative justice practitioners involves a comprehensive and multidimensional approach. A well-rounded curriculum includes theoretical knowledge, practical skills, and experiential learning opportunities, ensuring that practitioners are equipped to handle the complexities of restorative justice processes effectively. This chapter explores the key components of curriculum development, emphasizing the importance of ethical guidelines and reflective practice.

Theoretical Foundations

A solid theoretical foundation is essential for restorative justice practitioners. Understanding the underlying principles and philosophies of restorative justice provides the context and rationale for various practices and interventions.

Key Theoretical Components:

1. Introduction to Restorative Justice:

- Historical Development: An overview of the historical development of restorative justice, including its roots in indigenous practices and its evolution within modern justice systems.

- Core Principles: Understanding the core principles of restorative justice, such as repairing harm, involving stakeholders, and promoting healing and reconciliation.

2. Restorative Justice Models and Practices:

- Different Models: Exploring various models of restorative justice, such as victim-offender mediation, family group conferencing, and restorative circles.

- Case Studies: Analyzing case studies to illustrate the application of different models in various contexts and their outcomes.

3. Legal and Ethical Frameworks:

- Legal Context: Understanding the legal context within which restorative justice operates, including relevant laws, policies, and regulations.

- Ethical Considerations: Exploring ethical considerations, such as confidentiality, impartiality, and the rights of participants, to ensure ethical practice.

Practical Skills

Developing practical skills is crucial for restorative justice practitioners. These skills enable practitioners to facilitate restorative processes effectively and address the needs of participants.

Key Practical Skills:

1. Communication Skills:

- Active Listening: Techniques for active listening, including reflective listening, paraphrasing, and summarizing, to ensure participants feel heard and understood.

- Non-Verbal Communication: Understanding the role of non-verbal communication in mediation, such as body language, eye contact, and tone of voice.

2. Conflict Resolution:

- Conflict Analysis: Tools and techniques for analyzing conflicts, identifying underlying issues, and understanding the perspectives of all parties involved.

- De-Escalation Strategies: Strategies for de-escalating tense situations and managing emotions to maintain a constructive dialogue.

3. Facilitation Techniques:

- Guiding Dialogue: Techniques for guiding dialogue and ensuring that all participants have an opportunity to speak and contribute to the process.

- Building Consensus: Methods for building consensus and helping participants reach mutually acceptable agreements.

Experiential Learning Opportunities

Experiential learning opportunities provide practitioners with hands-on experience and practical application of theoretical knowledge and skills.

Key Experiential Learning Components:

1. Role-Playing Exercises:

- Simulated Mediation: Engaging in simulated mediation sessions to practice facilitation techniques, conflict resolution skills, and communication strategies.

- Feedback and Reflection: Receiving feedback from peers and instructors, and reflecting on performance to identify areas for improvement.

2. Supervised Practice:

- Mentorship Programs: Participating in mentorship programs where experienced practitioners provide guidance and support to novice practitioners.

- Field Experience: Gaining field experience through internships or placements with restorative justice organizations to observe and participate in real-world cases.

3. Workshops and Seminars:

- Specialized Training: Attending workshops and seminars on specialized topics, such as trauma-informed practice, cultural competency, and restorative justice in specific contexts (e.g., schools, prisons, communities).

- Interactive Learning: Engaging in interactive learning activities, such as group discussions, case study analysis, and problem-solving exercises.

Ethical Guidelines

Ethical guidelines are fundamental to the practice of restorative justice. Practitioners must adhere to these guidelines to ensure that their practice is ethical, respectful, and fair.

Key Ethical Guidelines:

1. Confidentiality:

- Respecting Privacy: Maintaining the confidentiality of information shared during restorative processes to protect the privacy of participants.

- Legal Obligations: Understanding the legal obligations and exceptions to confidentiality, such as mandatory reporting requirements.

2. Impartiality:

- Neutral Facilitation: Ensuring that practitioners remain neutral and impartial, avoiding any appearance of bias or favoritism.

- Equal Treatment: Treating all participants with respect and fairness, ensuring that everyone has an equal opportunity to participate and be heard.

3. Informed Consent:

- Voluntary Participation: Ensuring that participation in restorative processes is voluntary and based on informed consent.

- Transparency: Providing clear and comprehensive information about the process, including its purpose, procedures, and potential outcomes.

Reflective Practice

Reflective practice is essential for the continuous development and improvement of restorative justice practitioners. It involves regularly reflecting on experiences, identifying areas for growth, and making adjustments to improve practice.

Key Reflective Practice Components:

1. Self-Reflection:

- Personal Reflection: Engaging in personal reflection to examine one's own beliefs, biases, and assumptions, and their impact on practice.

- Reflective Journals: Keeping reflective journals to document experiences, challenges, and insights gained from practice.

2. Peer Reflection:

- Peer Feedback: Participating in peer feedback sessions to receive constructive feedback and support from colleagues.

- Group Reflection: Engaging in group reflection activities, such as case study discussions and debriefing sessions, to learn from shared experiences.

3. Continuous Improvement:

- Professional Development: Commit to ongoing professional development through training, workshops, and conferences to stay current with best practices and emerging trends.

- Adapting Practice: Using insights gained from reflection to adapt and improve practice, ensuring that it remains effective and responsive to participants' needs.

Developing a Comprehensive Curriculum

Developing a comprehensive curriculum for restorative justice practitioners involves integrating theoretical knowledge, practical skills, experiential learning opportunities, ethical guidelines, and reflective practice.

Curriculum Structure:

1. Foundation Courses:

- Introduction to Restorative Justice: Covering the history, principles, and models of restorative justice.

- Legal and Ethical Frameworks: Exploring the legal context and ethical considerations in restorative justice practice.

2. Skills Development Courses:

- Communication and Conflict Resolution: Developing communication skills and conflict resolution techniques.

- Facilitation and Mediation: Training in facilitation techniques and mediation practices.

3. Experiential Learning Modules:

- Role-Playing and Simulations: Engaging in role-playing exercises and simulated mediation sessions.

- Field Experience and Internships: Providing opportunities for supervised practice and field experience.

4. Ethics and Reflective Practice Courses:

- Ethical Guidelines: Exploring ethical principles and guidelines for restorative justice practitioners.

- Reflective Practice: Developing reflective practice skills through personal and peer reflection activities.

5. Specialized Training Modules:

- Trauma-Informed Practice: Training in trauma-informed approaches to restorative justice.

- Cultural Competency: Developing cultural competency skills to work effectively with diverse populations.

- Restorative Justice in Specific Contexts: Exploring the application of restorative justice in various settings, such as schools, prisons, and communities.

Conclusion

Developing comprehensive curricula for training restorative justice practitioners is essential for ensuring that they are equipped with the theoretical knowledge, practical skills, and ethical frameworks needed to facilitate effective restorative processes. By integrating foundational courses, skills development, experiential learning opportunities, ethical guidelines, and reflective practice, training programs can prepare practitioners to handle the complexities of restorative justice with competence and compassion. Continuous professional development and a commitment to reflective practice ensure that practitioners remain responsive to the needs of participants and adaptable to evolving best practices.

Through rigorous training and education, restorative justice practitioners can contribute to the creation of a more just and compassionate society.

Continuing Education and Certification

Continuing education and certification are vital components for maintaining high standards in restorative justice practice. Ongoing professional development ensures that practitioners remain updated on best practices, emerging research, and evolving ethical considerations. This chapter explores the importance of continuing education and certification, the types of educational opportunities available, the benefits of certification, and the process for achieving and maintaining certification.

The Importance of Continuing Education

Continuing education is essential for restorative justice practitioners to ensure that they stay current with the latest developments in the field. It fosters continuous improvement and professional growth, enabling practitioners to provide the highest quality of service.

Key Reasons for Continuing Education:

1. Staying Updated on Best Practices:

- Emerging Techniques: Learning about new mediation techniques, tools, and methodologies that enhance the effectiveness of restorative justice processes.

- Case Studies and Examples: Analyzing recent case studies and examples to understand successful applications and innovative approaches.

2. Understanding Emerging Research:

- Evidence-Based Practices: Incorporating findings from the latest research to adopt evidence-based practices that improve outcomes for participants.

- Research Collaboration: Engaging in collaborative research projects to contribute to the body of knowledge in restorative justice.

3. Adapting to Evolving Ethical Considerations:

- Ethical Dilemmas: Exploring evolving ethical dilemmas and developing strategies to navigate complex situations.

- Updated Guidelines: Staying informed about updated ethical guidelines and standards to ensure ethical practice.

4. Enhancing Professional Skills:

- Advanced Training: Participating in advanced training programs to develop specialized skills and knowledge.

- Peer Learning: Engaging in peer learning opportunities to share experiences and learn from colleagues.

Types of Continuing Education Opportunities

There are various continuing education opportunities available for restorative justice practitioners. These opportunities allow practitioners to pursue professional development in ways that best suit their needs and interests.

Workshops and Seminars:

- Topic-Specific Workshops: Attending workshops focused on specific topics such as trauma-informed practice, cultural competency, or advanced mediation techniques.

- Interactive Seminars: Participating in interactive seminars that provide hands-on learning experiences and foster collaborative discussions.

Conferences and Symposiums:

- National and International Conferences: Attending conferences to learn from leading experts, engage in networking opportunities, and stay updated on global trends in restorative justice.

- Symposiums: Participating in symposiums that focus on particular aspects of restorative justice, such as juvenile justice or community-based practices.

Online Courses and Webinars:

- Flexible Learning: Enroll in online courses and webinars that offer flexibility and convenience for busy professionals.

- Diverse Topics: Exploring a wide range of topics, from foundational principles to advanced restorative justice practices.

Professional Associations and Networks:

- Membership Benefits: Joining professional associations and networks that offer continuing education resources, such as journals, newsletters, and exclusive training opportunities.

- Peer Support: Engaging in peer support and mentorship programs facilitated by professional associations.

Academic Programs:

- Advanced Degrees: Pursuing advanced degrees, such as master's or doctoral programs, in restorative justice or related fields.

- Certificate Programs: Enrolling in academic certificate programs that provide specialized training and credentials.

The Benefits of Certification

Certification in restorative justice practice provides numerous benefits for practitioners, participants, and the broader community. It signifies a commitment to professional excellence and adherence to high standards.

Key Benefits of Certification:

1. Professional Credibility:

- Recognition: Certification is a mark of professional recognition and credibility, enhancing practitioners' reputations within the field.

- Standards of Practice: Certified practitioners are recognized for adhering to established standards of practice and ethical guidelines.

2. Enhanced Competence:

- Skill Development: The certification process ensures that practitioners have developed the necessary skills and knowledge to conduct restorative justice processes effectively.

- Continuous Improvement: Certification encourages ongoing professional development and continuous improvement.

3. Increased Opportunities:

- Career Advancement: Certification can open up career advancement opportunities, such as leadership roles, consultancy positions, or specialized practice areas.

- Networking: Certified practitioners often have access to professional networks and resources that facilitate collaboration and career growth.

4. Participant Confidence:

- Trust and Confidence: Certification instills trust and confidence in participants, ensuring that they receive high-quality and ethical restorative justice services.

- Quality Assurance: Participants can be assured that certified practitioners are committed to maintaining high standards of practice.

The Certification Process

Achieving and maintaining certification in restorative justice practice involves several key steps. These steps ensure that practitioners meet rigorous standards and are committed to continuous professional development.

Steps to Certification:

1. Eligibility Requirements:

- Educational Background: Meeting the educational requirements, such as a degree in a related field or completion of specific training programs.

- Professional Experience: Accumulating relevant professional experience in restorative justice practice.

2. Application Process:

- Documentation: Submitting documentation of educational qualifications, professional experience, and completed training programs.

- References: Providing references from colleagues, mentors, or supervisors who can attest to the applicant's skills and ethical practice.

3. Examination:

- Written Exam: Successfully completing a written examination that tests theoretical knowledge, practical skills, and ethical understanding.

- Practical Assessment: Participating in a practical assessment, such as a simulated mediation session, to demonstrate applied skills.

4. Certification Award:

- Review Process: Undergoing a review process conducted by a certification board or professional association to ensure all requirements are met.

- Certification Issuance: Receiving official certification upon successful completion of the application and examination process.

Maintaining Certification:

1. Continuing Education Requirements:

- Ongoing Training: Completing a specified number of continuing education hours or units within a set period to maintain certification.

- Approved Programs: Participating in approved continuing education programs, workshops, conferences, or courses.

2. Renewal Process:

- Regular Renewal: Submitting a renewal application, typically every few years, along with documentation of continuing education and professional development activities.

- Reassessment: Undergoing periodic reassessment or recertification to ensure continued adherence to standards and ethical guidelines.

3. Ethical Practice:

- Adherence to Guidelines: Maintaining adherence to ethical guidelines and standards of practice set by the certifying body.

- Professional Conduct: Demonstrating ongoing professional conduct that aligns with the principles of restorative justice.

Conclusion

Continuing education and certification are vital for maintaining high standards in restorative justice practice. Ongoing professional development ensures that practitioners stay updated on best practices, emerging research, and evolving ethical considerations. Certification provides professional credibility, enhances competence, increases career opportunities, and instills confidence in participants. The certification process involves meeting eligibility requirements, completing an application and examination process, and committing to continuous education and ethical practice. By investing in continuing education and certification, restorative justice practitioners can ensure they provide the highest quality of service, contributing to the effectiveness and integrity of restorative justice processes and promoting a more just and compassionate society.

Training and Education for Practitioners

Building a Community of Practice

Building a community of practice involves creating networks and platforms for restorative justice practitioners to share knowledge, resources, and support. This community fosters collaboration, innovation, and collective growth, enhancing the overall impact of restorative justice. This chapter explores the importance of building a community of practice, strategies for developing and sustaining such communities, and the benefits they provide to practitioners and the broader field of restorative justice.

The Importance of Building a Community of Practice

A community of practice offers significant benefits for restorative justice practitioners and the field as a whole. It provides a supportive environment for continuous learning, sharing experiences, and collectively addressing challenges.

Key Reasons for Building a Community of Practice:

1. Fostering Collaboration:

- Knowledge Sharing: Practitioners can share insights, strategies, and best practices, enhancing collective expertise.

- Collaborative Projects: Opportunities for joint research, policy advocacy, and program development can emerge from collaborative efforts.

2. Promoting Innovation:

- Creative Solutions: A community of practice encourages creative problem-solving and the development of innovative approaches to restorative justice.

- Adaptation and Flexibility: Practitioners can adapt successful strategies from diverse contexts to meet local needs.

3. Enhancing Professional Growth:

- Peer Learning: Learning from peers through discussions, workshops, and mentorship accelerates professional development.

- Reflective Practice: Engaging in reflective practice with peers helps practitioners critically evaluate their work and improve their skills.

4. Providing Support and Resources:

- Emotional Support: A supportive community offers emotional support, reducing isolation and burnout among practitioners.

- Access to Resources: Sharing resources, such as training materials, research findings, and funding opportunities, enhances practitioners' capacity to deliver effective services.

Strategies for Developing and Sustaining a Community of Practice

Developing and sustaining a community of practice requires intentional efforts to create networks, facilitate communication, and foster a sense of belonging among practitioners.

1. Establishing Networks and Platforms:

1. Professional Associations:

- Membership Networks: Joining professional associations dedicated to restorative justice creates a formal network of practitioners.

- Annual Conferences: Organizing and attending annual conferences provides opportunities for face-to-face networking and knowledge exchange.

2. Online Platforms:

- Forums and Discussion Groups: Creating online forums and discussion groups allows practitioners to connect and share insights regardless of geographical location.

- Social Media: Utilizing social media platforms to create groups and pages dedicated to restorative justice fosters real-time communication and engagement.

3. Local and Regional Networks:

- Regional Chapters: Establishing regional chapters of professional associations or informal local networks facilitates closer collaboration and support.

- Community Meetings: Organizing regular community meetings or gatherings provides opportunities for practitioners to connect and share experiences.

2. Facilitating Communication and Collaboration:

1. Regular Meetings and Webinars:

- Monthly Webinars: Hosting monthly webinars on various topics related to restorative justice keeps practitioners informed and engaged.

- Virtual Coffee Chats: Organizing informal virtual coffee chats encourages casual conversations and relationship-building.

2. Collaborative Projects and Working Groups:

- Research Collaborations: Forming working groups to collaborate on research projects enhances the evidence base for restorative justice practices.

- Policy Advocacy: Joint efforts in policy advocacy can amplify the collective voice of practitioners and influence legislative changes.

3. Resource Sharing:

- Resource Libraries: Creating online resource libraries with training materials, research articles, and practical tools provides valuable support to practitioners.

- Knowledge Hubs: Establishing knowledge hubs where practitioners can contribute and access resources fosters a culture of sharing and continuous learning.

3. Fostering a Sense of Belonging:

1. Inclusive Practices:

- Diverse Representation: Ensuring diverse representation within the community of practice promotes inclusivity and broadens perspectives.

- Cultural Sensitivity: Practicing cultural sensitivity and respect for different approaches and traditions enriches the community.

2. Mentorship Programs:

- Peer Mentorship: Establishing peer mentorship programs pairs experienced practitioners with newcomers, providing guidance and support.

- Formal Mentorship: Creating formal mentorship opportunities through professional associations enhances structured learning and development.

3. Recognition and Celebration:

- Awards and Acknowledgments: Recognizing and celebrating the achievements and contributions of practitioners fosters a sense of pride and belonging.

- Success Stories: Sharing success stories and case studies within the community highlights the impact of restorative justice and inspires continued efforts.

Benefits of a Community of Practice

A well-developed community of practice offers numerous benefits to individual practitioners and the broader field of restorative justice.

1. Enhanced Learning and Development:

- Continuous Education: Access to ongoing educational opportunities and resources supports continuous professional development.

- Skill Enhancement: Collaborative learning and peer feedback enhance practitioners' skills and competencies.

2. Increased Collaboration and Innovation:

- Shared Expertise: Collaborative projects and knowledge sharing leverage collective expertise to address complex challenges.

- Innovative Approaches: Exposure to diverse perspectives and practices fosters innovation and the development of new strategies.

3. Strengthened Professional Identity:

- Sense of Community: Belonging to a community of practice strengthens practitioners' professional identity and commitment to restorative justice.

- Shared Values: Emphasizing shared values and principles reinforces the collective mission and vision of restorative justice.

4. Improved Practice and Outcomes:

- Quality Assurance: Regular interaction and feedback within the community promote high standards of practice and continuous improvement.

- Positive Impact: Enhanced skills, knowledge, and collaboration contribute to better outcomes for participants and communities.

Case Study: A Successful Community of Practice

Background:

- The Restorative Justice Network (RJN) is a global community of practice established to support restorative justice practitioners worldwide.

Development and Strategies:

- Establishment: RJN was established by a group of restorative justice leaders who recognized the need for a global platform to share knowledge and resources.

- Online Platform: An online platform was created, featuring forums, resource libraries, and a calendar of events.

- Regular Engagement: Monthly webinars, virtual coffee chats, and annual conferences were organized to facilitate regular engagement and collaboration.

- Mentorship Program: A peer mentorship program was launched, pairing experienced practitioners with newcomers.

Outcomes and Benefits:

- Knowledge Sharing: RJN facilitated the sharing of best practices, research findings, and innovative approaches among practitioners.

- Collaborative Projects: Several collaborative research projects and policy advocacy initiatives emerged from the network.

- Professional Growth: Practitioners reported enhanced skills, increased confidence, and a stronger sense of professional identity.

- Global Impact: RJN's efforts contributed to the growth and development of restorative justice practices globally, benefiting diverse communities.

Conclusion

Building a community of practice for restorative justice practitioners is essential for fostering collaboration, innovation, and collective growth. By establishing networks and platforms for knowledge sharing, facilitating communication and collaboration, and fostering a sense of belonging, practitioners can enhance their professional development and the overall impact of restorative justice. The benefits of a well-developed community of practice include enhanced learning and development, increased collaboration and innovation, strengthened professional identity, and improved practice and outcomes. Through intentional efforts to build and sustain these communities, restorative justice practitioners can contribute to a more just and compassionate society, continually improving their practice and expanding the reach and effectiveness of restorative justice.

CHAPTER 10

CHALLENGES AND CRITICISM

Addressing Skepticism and Resistance

Restorative justice faces skepticism and resistance from various quarters, including traditional justice systems, policymakers, and the public. Addressing these challenges involves advocacy, education, and demonstrating the effectiveness of restorative justice through evidence-based practices. This chapter explores the sources of skepticism and resistance, strategies for addressing these challenges, and the importance of advocacy and education in promoting restorative justice.

Sources of Skepticism and Resistance

Skepticism and resistance to restorative justice can stem from a variety of sources. Understanding these sources is essential for developing effective strategies to address them.

1. Traditional Justice Systems:

- Retributive Focus: Traditional justice systems are often rooted in retributive justice, which emphasizes punishment over rehabilitation and reconciliation.

- Institutional Inertia: Established systems and procedures can be resistant to change, making it difficult to integrate restorative practices.

- Perceived Softness: Restorative justice may be viewed as too lenient or "soft" on crime, leading to skepticism about its effectiveness in deterring criminal behavior.

2. Policymakers:

- Lack of Awareness: Policymakers may lack awareness or understanding of restorative justice principles and their benefits.

- Political Considerations: Political pressures and the desire to appear tough on crime can lead to resistance against adopting restorative justice practices.

- Resource Allocation: Concerns about the costs and resource requirements of implementing restorative justice programs can hinder support.

3. The Public:

- Misconceptions: The public may hold misconceptions about restorative justice, viewing it as forgiving or excusing criminal behavior.

- Fear and Safety Concerns: Fears about public safety and the potential for recidivism can lead to resistance against restorative approaches.

- Cultural Attitudes: Cultural attitudes toward crime and punishment can influence public perceptions and acceptance of restorative justice.

Strategies for Addressing Challenges

Effectively addressing skepticism and resistance to restorative justice requires a multifaceted approach that includes advocacy, education, and evidence-based practices.

1. Advocacy and Education:

1. Raising Awareness:

- Public Campaigns: Launching public awareness campaigns to educate the public about restorative justice principles, benefits, and success stories.

- Media Engagement: Utilizing media outlets to share positive outcomes and personal testimonials from restorative justice participants.

2. Engaging Stakeholders:

- Workshops and Seminars: Organizing workshops and seminars for policymakers, legal professionals, and community leaders to provide comprehensive information about restorative justice.

- Stakeholder Meetings: Facilitating meetings and discussions with key stakeholders to address concerns and highlight the effectiveness of restorative approaches.

3. Educational Programs:

- School Curricula: Integrating restorative justice concepts into school curricula to educate young people about alternative approaches to conflict resolution.

- Professional Training: Offering training programs for legal professionals, law enforcement, and social workers to build understanding and support for restorative practices.

2. Demonstrating Effectiveness Through Evidence-Based Practices:

1. Collecting Data:

- Program Evaluation: Conducting rigorous evaluations of restorative justice programs to collect data on outcomes such as recidivism rates, victim satisfaction, and community impact.

- Comparative Studies: Comparing restorative justice outcomes with those of traditional justice approaches to highlight the benefits and effectiveness of restorative practices.

2. Publishing Research:

- Academic Journals: Publishing research findings in academic journals to build a robust evidence base and gain credibility within the academic and professional communities.

- Policy Briefs: Developing policy briefs and reports that summarize research findings and make a compelling case for the adoption of restorative justice practices.

3. Showcasing Success Stories:

- Case Studies: Sharing detailed case studies that illustrate the positive impact of restorative justice on individuals and communities.

- Personal Testimonials: Highlighting personal testimonials from victims, offenders, and community members who have experienced the benefits of restorative justice.

3. Building Collaborative Partnerships:

1. Cross-Sector Collaboration:

- Partnerships with Law Enforcement: Collaborating with law enforcement agencies to integrate restorative practices into policing and community relations.

- Judicial Support: Engaging judges and court personnel to support the implementation of restorative justice programs within the judicial system.

2. Community Involvement:

- Grassroots Organizations: Partnering with grassroots organizations and community groups to promote restorative justice at the local level.

- Volunteer Programs: Developing volunteer programs that involve community members in restorative justice processes, such as serving as mediators or support persons.

3. Interagency Coordination:

- Coordinated Services: Coordinating with social services, mental health agencies, and educational institutions to provide comprehensive support for restorative justice participants.

- Integrated Approaches: Creating integrated approaches that combine restorative justice with other interventions, such as substance abuse treatment or mental health counseling.

Addressing Specific Concerns

To effectively address skepticism and resistance, it is important to address specific concerns raised by different stakeholders.

1. Concerns About Effectiveness:

- Recidivism Rates: Providing evidence that restorative justice reduces recidivism rates compared to traditional punitive approaches.

- Victim Satisfaction: Highlighting high levels of victim satisfaction and healing achieved through restorative justice processes.

2. Concerns About Public Safety:

- Risk Assessment: Implementing thorough risk assessment procedures to ensure that restorative justice is used appropriately and does not compromise public safety.

- Monitoring and Support: Providing ongoing monitoring and support for offenders participating in restorative justice programs to prevent reoffending.

3. Concerns About Costs and Resources:

- Cost-Effectiveness: Demonstrating that restorative justice can be cost-effective by reducing the burden on the criminal justice system and lowering incarceration rates.

- Resource Allocation: Advocating for the allocation of resources to restorative justice programs, highlighting potential long-term savings and social benefits.

4. Cultural and Attitudinal Barriers:

- Cultural Sensitivity: Ensuring that restorative justice programs are culturally sensitive and tailored to the needs of diverse communities.

- Changing Attitudes: Promoting a shift in cultural attitudes toward crime and punishment through education and awareness-raising efforts.

Case Study: Overcoming Resistance in a Local Community

Background:

- A local community faced significant resistance to the implementation of a restorative justice program for juvenile offenders. Concerns were raised by law enforcement, school officials, and parents about the program's effectiveness and impact on public safety.

Strategies Employed:

1. Advocacy and Education:

- Public Forums: Organized public forums and town hall meetings to educate the community about restorative justice principles and address concerns.

- School Workshops: Conducted workshops in schools to educate students, teachers, and parents about restorative justice and its benefits.

2. Demonstrating Effectiveness:

- Pilot Program Evaluation: Implemented a pilot program and conducted a rigorous evaluation to collect data on outcomes, such as recidivism rates and participant satisfaction.

- Success Stories: Shared success stories from similar programs in other communities to build confidence and support.

3. Building Partnerships:

- Law Enforcement Collaboration: Partnered with local law enforcement to integrate restorative justice into juvenile diversion programs.

- Community Involvement: Involved community members in the planning and implementation of the program to ensure it met local needs and gained broader support.

Outcomes:

- Increased Support: As a result of these efforts, resistance decreased, and support for the program grew among community members, law enforcement, and school officials.

- Positive Impact: The pilot program demonstrated positive outcomes, including reduced recidivism rates and high levels of participant satisfaction, leading to its expansion and long-term sustainability.

Conclusion

Addressing skepticism and resistance to restorative justice involves a comprehensive approach that includes advocacy, education, and demonstrating the effectiveness of restorative practices through evidence-based approaches. By raising awareness, engaging stakeholders, and building collaborative partnerships, restorative justice practitioners can overcome resistance and promote the adoption of restorative approaches within traditional justice systems and the broader community. Addressing specific concerns about effectiveness, public safety, costs, and cultural attitudes is essential for gaining support and ensuring the success of restorative justice programs. Through persistent efforts and a commitment to education and advocacy, restorative justice can continue to grow and make a positive impact on individuals and communities, promoting healing, reconciliation, and a more just society.

Challenges and Criticisms

Overcoming Systemic Barriers

Systemic barriers such as funding limitations, institutional resistance, and policy gaps can significantly hinder the implementation and sustainability of restorative justice programs. Addressing these barriers requires strategic planning, stakeholder engagement, and robust advocacy efforts. This chapter explores the various systemic barriers to restorative justice, strategies to overcome them, and the importance of a coordinated approach to promote and sustain restorative justice initiatives.

Identifying Systemic Barriers

To effectively overcome systemic barriers, it is essential first to identify and understand the nature of these obstacles.

1. Funding Limitations:

- Budget Constraints: Limited financial resources can restrict the development, implementation, and expansion of restorative justice programs.

- Competing Priorities: Allocating funds to restorative justice programs can be challenging when competing with other priorities within the justice system and community services.

2. Institutional Resistance:

- Entrenched Practices: Traditional justice systems may resist adopting restorative practices due to established procedures and a focus on retributive justice.

- Lack of Awareness: Institutional resistance can stem from a lack of awareness or understanding of the benefits and principles of restorative justice.

3. Policy Gaps:

- Inadequate Legislation: Gaps in legislation and policy frameworks can hinder the formal integration of restorative justice into the criminal justice system.

- Lack of Guidelines: The absence of clear guidelines and standards for restorative justice practices can lead to inconsistency and reluctance to adopt these approaches.

Strategies for Overcoming Systemic Barriers

Addressing systemic barriers to restorative justice requires a comprehensive and strategic approach. The following strategies can help overcome these obstacles:

1. Securing Funding and Resources:

1. Advocacy and Awareness Campaigns:

- Highlighting Benefits: Conduct campaigns to raise awareness about the social, economic, and rehabilitative benefits of restorative justice, targeting policymakers, funders, and the public.

- Success Stories: Share success stories and case studies that demonstrate the positive outcomes and cost-effectiveness of restorative justice programs.

2. Diversifying Funding Sources:

- Government Grants: Apply for government grants dedicated to criminal justice reform, community development, and mental health services.

- Philanthropic Support: Seek funding from philanthropic organizations and foundations that support social justice, community healing, and innovative justice practices.

- Community Contributions: Encourage community contributions through crowdfunding, donations, and local fundraising events.

3. Cost-Benefit Analysis:

- Economic Impact Studies: Conduct and present cost-benefit analyses that highlight the long-term savings and social benefits of restorative justice compared to traditional punitive approaches.

- Policy Briefs: Develop policy briefs that outline the financial and social advantages of investing in restorative justice programs.

2. Addressing Institutional Resistance:

1. Education and Training:

- Workshops and Seminars: Organize workshops and seminars for legal professionals, law enforcement, and corrections officers to educate them on the principles and benefits of restorative justice.

- Professional Development: Incorporate restorative justice training into professional development programs for judges, prosecutors, defense attorneys, and other justice system personnel.

2. Building Alliances:

- Cross-Sector Collaboration: Establish alliances with various sectors, including education, healthcare, social services, and community organizations, to build broad-based support for restorative justice.

- Champion Leaders: Identify and support leaders within the justice system who advocate for restorative justice, leveraging their influence to promote change.

3. Pilot Programs:

- Demonstration Projects: Implement pilot programs to showcase the effectiveness of restorative justice in specific contexts, such as juvenile justice, schools, or community disputes.

- Evaluation and Reporting: Conduct thorough evaluations of pilot programs and share the results with stakeholders to build credibility and support for broader implementation.

3. Closing Policy Gaps:

1. Policy Advocacy:

- Legislative Proposals: Develop and advocate for legislative proposals that support the integration of restorative justice into the criminal justice system.

- Policy Recommendations: Provide policymakers with evidence-based recommendations for creating supportive policy frameworks and guidelines for restorative justice practices.

2. Developing Standards and Guidelines:

- Best Practices: Develop and disseminate best practice guidelines for restorative justice programs, ensuring consistency and quality across different contexts.

- Accreditation and Certification: Establish accreditation and certification processes for restorative justice practitioners and programs to standardize practices and enhance credibility.

3. Engaging Policymakers:

- Policy Briefings: Conduct briefings and presentations for policymakers to educate them on the benefits and implementation strategies for restorative justice.

- Stakeholder Roundtables: Organize roundtable discussions with key stakeholders, including legislators, justice system officials, community leaders, and restorative justice practitioners, to build consensus and support for policy changes.

Case Study: Overcoming Systemic Barriers in a Regional Restorative Justice Program

Background:

- A regional restorative justice program faced significant barriers, including limited funding, resistance from traditional justice institutions, and gaps in policy support. Despite these challenges, the program successfully implemented restorative practices through strategic efforts.

Strategies Employed:

1. Securing Funding and Resources:

- Philanthropic Grants: The program secured grants from local philanthropic foundations that supported community-based justice initiatives.

- Government Support: Advocacy efforts led to government funding for a pilot program, highlighting the program's potential for reducing recidivism and promoting community healing.

2. Addressing Institutional Resistance:

- Education Workshops: The program organized workshops for judges, prosecutors, and law enforcement officers, demonstrating the effectiveness of restorative justice through case studies and expert presentations.

- Pilot Success: A successful pilot program in juvenile justice showcased significant reductions in reoffending rates, garnering support from skeptical justice officials.

3. Closing Policy Gaps:

- Legislative Advocacy: Program leaders worked with policymakers to draft and advocate for legislation that formally recognized and supported restorative justice practices.

- Developing Guidelines: The program developed comprehensive guidelines and best practices, which were adopted by local justice institutions to standardize restorative practices.

Outcomes:

- Increased Funding: The program secured ongoing funding from both governmental and non-governmental sources, ensuring its sustainability.

- Institutional Support: Resistance from traditional justice institutions decreased as they observed the positive outcomes of restorative justice, leading to broader acceptance and integration.

- Policy Changes: New legislation and policy guidelines provided a supportive framework for the continued growth and implementation of restorative justice programs in the region.

Conclusion

Overcoming systemic barriers to restorative justice requires strategic planning, stakeholder engagement, and robust advocacy efforts. By securing funding and resources, addressing institutional resistance, and closing policy gaps, restorative justice practitioners can promote and sustain effective restorative practices. A coordinated approach that includes education, collaboration, and evidence-based advocacy is essential for addressing skepticism and resistance, ultimately leading to a more just and compassionate justice system. Through persistent efforts and a commitment to systemic change, restorative justice can become a mainstream approach, promoting healing, reconciliation, and community well-being.

Evaluating Effectiveness and Impact

Evaluating the effectiveness and impact of restorative justice programs is crucial for their continued development, support, and credibility. Comprehensive evaluation involves using both quantitative and qualitative methods to assess outcomes, identify areas for improvement, and build a robust evidence base. This chapter explores the importance of evaluation, the various methods and tools used, and the key indicators of success in restorative justice programs.

The Importance of Evaluation

Evaluation plays a critical role in the development and sustainability of restorative justice programs. It helps practitioners and stakeholders understand the strengths and weaknesses of their initiatives and provides evidence to support ongoing investment and expansion.

Key Reasons for Evaluation:

1. Demonstrating Effectiveness:

- Evidence-Based Practice: Providing empirical evidence of the positive outcomes of restorative justice programs enhances their credibility and supports their adoption.

- Stakeholder Confidence: Demonstrating effectiveness builds confidence among stakeholders, including policymakers, funders, and the community.

2. Continuous Improvement:

- Identifying Strengths and Weaknesses: Evaluation helps identify what works well and what needs improvement, guiding practitioners in refining their practices.

- Adapting to Changes: Regular evaluation enables programs to adapt to changing needs and contexts, ensuring their continued relevance and effectiveness.

3. Accountability:

- Transparency: Evaluation promotes transparency and accountability, showing how resources are used and what impacts are achieved.

- Meeting Goals: Assessing whether programs meet their intended goals and objectives is essential for justifying continued funding and support.

4. Policy Development:

- Informing Policy: Evaluation findings can inform policy development, providing a strong evidence base for legislative and policy changes that support restorative justice.

Methods and Tools for Evaluation

Evaluating restorative justice programs involves using a combination of quantitative and qualitative methods to capture a comprehensive picture of their effectiveness and impact.

1. Quantitative Methods:

1. Surveys and Questionnaires:

- Pre- and Post-Participation Surveys: Conducting surveys before and after participation to measure changes in attitudes, behaviors, and perceptions.

- Standardized Instruments: Using standardized instruments to assess specific outcomes, such as recidivism rates, victim satisfaction, and community trust.

2. Statistical Analysis:

- Recidivism Rates: Analyzing recidivism rates among offenders who participate in restorative justice programs compared to those who do not.

- Cost-Benefit Analysis: Conducting cost-benefit analyses to compare the economic impacts of restorative justice programs with traditional justice approaches.

3. Data Collection:

- Administrative Data: Collecting data from program records, justice system databases, and other administrative sources to track outcomes and trends.

- Longitudinal Studies: Implementing longitudinal studies to assess the long-term impacts of restorative justice on participants and communities.

2. Qualitative Methods:

1. Interviews:

- In-Depth Interviews: Conduct in-depth interviews with participants, including victims, offenders, and facilitators, to gain insights into their experiences and perceptions.

- Key Informant Interviews: Engaging key informants, such as community leaders, justice officials, and policymakers, to gather perspectives on the broader impact of restorative justice.

2. Focus Groups:

- Participant Focus Groups: Organizing focus groups with participants to discuss their experiences, challenges, and suggestions for improvement.

- Stakeholder Focus Groups: Facilitating focus groups with stakeholders to explore their views on the effectiveness and implementation of restorative justice programs.

3. Case Studies:

- Detailed Case Analyses: Developing detailed case studies that highlight specific examples of restorative justice in action, illustrating processes, outcomes, and lessons learned.

- Narrative Accounts: Collect narrative accounts from participants to provide a rich, contextual understanding of the restorative justice experience.

3. Mixed-Methods Approaches:

1. Combining Quantitative and Qualitative Data:

- Integrated Evaluation Designs: Using mixed-methods approaches that combine quantitative and qualitative data to provide a comprehensive evaluation.

- Triangulation: Triangulating data from multiple sources to validate findings and enhance the reliability of the evaluation.

Key Indicators of Success

Effective evaluation involves assessing a range of indicators that reflect the success and impact of restorative justice programs. These indicators can be categorized into immediate, intermediate, and long-term outcomes.

1. Immediate Outcomes:

1. Participant Satisfaction:

- Victim Satisfaction: Measuring the satisfaction of victims with the restorative justice process and their sense of justice and closure.

- Offender Satisfaction: Assessing offenders' satisfaction with the process and their sense of accountability and remorse.

2. Process Effectiveness:

- Facilitation Quality: Evaluating the quality of facilitation, including the mediator's skills, impartiality, and ability to foster a safe and respectful dialogue.

- Participation Rates: Tracking participation rates to understand the reach and accessibility of the program.

2. Intermediate Outcomes:

1. Behavioral Changes:

- Recidivism Reduction: Measuring reductions in reoffending rates among offenders who participate in restorative justice programs.

- Behavioral Improvements: Assessing improvements in offenders' behavior, such as increased empathy, responsibility, and commitment to positive change.

2. Emotional and Psychological Impact:

- Victim Healing: Evaluating the emotional and psychological healing of victims, including reductions in trauma symptoms and increases in feelings of safety and empowerment.

- Offender Rehabilitation: Assessing the rehabilitation of offenders, including their engagement in positive activities and relationships.

3. Community Impact:

- Community Trust: Measuring changes in community trust and cohesion, including perceptions of fairness and safety.

- Social Capital: Assessing increases in social capital, such as stronger community networks and support systems.

3. Long-Term Outcomes:

1. Sustainable Change:

- Long-Term Recidivism: Tracking long-term recidivism rates to assess the sustained impact of restorative justice on reducing criminal behavior.

- Continued Engagement: Evaluating participants' continued engagement in positive behaviors and community activities.

2. Systemic Impact:

- Policy Changes: Assessing the impact of restorative justice programs on policy and legislative changes that support restorative practices.

- Institutional Adoption: Evaluating the integration of restorative justice into traditional justice systems and institutional practices.

3. Broad Social Impact:

- Crime Rates: Analyzing changes in overall crime rates within communities that have implemented restorative justice programs.

- Public Perception: Measuring changes in public perception and support for restorative justice as a legitimate and effective approach to justice.

Case Study: Evaluating a Restorative Justice Program
Background:

- A restorative justice program implemented in a mid-sized city focused on juvenile offenders and aimed to reduce recidivism, promote victim healing, and strengthen community ties.

Evaluation Methods:

1. Quantitative Data Collection:

- Surveys: Pre- and post-participation surveys were administered to victims, offenders, and community members to measure satisfaction, perceptions of justice, and behavioral changes.

- Recidivism Tracking: Recidivism rates were tracked for participating offenders over a three-year period using justice system records.

2. Qualitative Data Collection:

- Interviews: In-depth interviews were conducted with victims, offenders, facilitators, and community leaders to gather detailed insights into their experiences and the program's impact.

- Focus Groups: Focus groups were held with participants and stakeholders to discuss the program's strengths, challenges, and areas for improvement.

Key Findings:

1. Immediate Outcomes:

- High Satisfaction Rates: Both victims and offenders reported high levels of satisfaction with the restorative justice process, citing fair treatment and meaningful dialogue.

- Effective Facilitation: Participants highlighted the quality of facilitation as a key factor in their positive experience.

2. Intermediate Outcomes:

- Significant Recidivism Reduction: The program achieved a significant reduction in recidivism rates among participating juvenile offenders compared to a control group.

- Emotional Healing: Victims reported substantial emotional healing, including reduced trauma symptoms and increased feelings of closure and empowerment.

3. Long-Term Outcomes:

- Sustained Behavioral Change: Offenders demonstrated sustained positive behavioral changes, including continued engagement in school and community activities.

- Policy Influence: The program's success influenced local policymakers to support the expansion of restorative justice initiatives and incorporate restorative principles into juvenile justice policies.

Conclusion:

- The evaluation demonstrated the program's effectiveness in achieving its goals and provided valuable insights for continuous improvement. The findings supported ongoing investment and policy changes, promoting the broader adoption of restorative justice practices.

Conclusion

Evaluating the effectiveness and impact of restorative justice programs is crucial for their continued development and support. Using quantitative and qualitative methods to assess outcomes, identify areas for improvement, and build a strong evidence base ensures that restorative justice practices remain relevant, effective, and credible. Key indicators of success, including participant satisfaction, behavioral changes, community impact, and long-term outcomes, provide a comprehensive picture of the program's impact. Through rigorous evaluation and continuous improvement, restorative justice can continue to grow and contribute to a more just and compassionate society, promoting healing, reconciliation, and positive change.

CHAPTER 11

FUTURE DIRECTIONS IN RESTORATIVE JUSTICE

Innovations in Practice

Innovations in restorative justice practice are continuously emerging, driven by research, technology, and evolving societal needs. Exploring these innovations provides insights into new approaches, tools, and methodologies that can enhance the impact of restorative justice. This chapter delves into the latest developments in restorative justice, highlighting key innovations that are transforming the field and expanding its reach and effectiveness.

Technological Advancements

Technological advancements are playing a significant role in the evolution of restorative justice practices. From virtual mediation platforms to data analytics, technology is opening new avenues for implementing and enhancing restorative justice.

1. Virtual Mediation Platforms:

1. Online Mediation:

- Accessibility: Virtual mediation platforms make restorative justice accessible to individuals who may face geographical, physical, or logistical barriers.

- Flexibility: Online mediation offers flexibility in scheduling and participation, allowing for greater convenience and inclusivity.

2. Digital Tools:

- Secure Communication: Utilizing secure digital tools ensures confidentiality and privacy during online mediation sessions.

- Resource Sharing: Virtual platforms enable easy sharing of resources, such as documents, videos, and educational materials, enhancing the mediation process.

2. Data Analytics and Artificial Intelligence:

1. Predictive Analytics:

- Identifying Trends: Data analytics can identify trends and patterns in restorative justice outcomes, helping practitioners refine their approaches and target interventions more effectively.

- Risk Assessment: Predictive analytics tools can assist in assessing the risk of recidivism and tailoring restorative justice programs to individual needs.

2. Artificial Intelligence:

- Automated Processes: AI-powered tools can automate administrative tasks, such as scheduling, case management, and data analysis, increasing efficiency.

- Enhanced Decision-Making: AI can provide insights and recommendations based on data analysis, supporting practitioners in making informed decisions.

Innovative Approaches

Innovative approaches in restorative justice are expanding its application and impact, addressing a wider range of conflicts and integrating restorative principles into various sectors.

1. Restorative Justice in Education:

1. Restorative Practices in Schools:

- School Climate: Implementing restorative practices in schools helps create a positive and inclusive school climate, reducing incidents of bullying and disciplinary issues.

- Peer Mediation: Training students as peer mediators empowers them to resolve conflicts among their peers, fostering a sense of responsibility and community.

2. Trauma-Informed Approaches:

- Understanding Trauma: Incorporating trauma-informed practices into restorative justice helps address the underlying trauma that may contribute to conflict and harmful behavior.

- Supportive Environment: Creating a supportive environment that recognizes and responds to trauma enhances the effectiveness of restorative justice interventions.

2. Restorative Justice in the Workplace:

1. Conflict Resolution:

- Workplace Mediation: Applying restorative justice principles in the workplace helps resolve conflicts, improve communication, and build a collaborative work environment.

- Employee Well-Being: Restorative practices promote employee well-being by addressing grievances and fostering a culture of respect and inclusivity.

2. Organizational Change:

- Restorative Culture: Building a restorative culture within organizations encourages transparency, accountability, and mutual support among employees.

- Leadership Development: Training leaders in restorative practices equips them with the skills to manage conflicts and promote a positive organizational culture.

3. Restorative Justice in the Criminal Justice System:

1. Restorative Policing:

- Community Engagement: Restorative policing practices focus on building trust and collaboration between law enforcement and the community, addressing the root causes of crime.

- Alternative Responses: Implementing restorative approaches as alternatives to traditional punitive measures helps reduce incarceration rates and promote rehabilitation.

2. Restorative Prisons:

- Prison Culture: Integrating restorative justice into prison culture supports the rehabilitation of inmates and reduces recidivism by fostering accountability and personal growth.

- Reentry Programs: Restorative reentry programs assist formerly incarcerated individuals in reintegrating into society, addressing the challenges they face and promoting successful transitions.

Methodological Innovations

Innovations in methodologies are enhancing the practice of restorative justice, making it more effective, inclusive, and adaptable to various contexts.

1. Holistic Approaches:

1. Integrative Practices:

- Combining Approaches: Integrating restorative justice with other approaches, such as transformative justice and community-based justice, creates a more comprehensive and flexible framework.

- Multidisciplinary Teams: Employing multidisciplinary teams, including social workers, psychologists, and community advocates, enriches the restorative process and addresses diverse needs.

2. Whole-Community Involvement:

- Community Circles: Expanding the use of community circles to involve a broader range of stakeholders in the restorative process enhances community cohesion and collective problem-solving.

- Inclusive Participation: Ensuring that restorative processes are inclusive and accessible to all community members, including marginalized and underrepresented groups, promotes equity and social justice.

2. Evidence-Based Practices:

1. Research and Evaluation:

- Rigorous Evaluation: Conducting rigorous evaluations of restorative justice programs using both quantitative and qualitative methods provides evidence of their effectiveness and informs best practices.

- Continuous Improvement: Utilizing evaluation findings to continuously improve and adapt restorative justice programs ensures their ongoing relevance and effectiveness.

2. Standardization and Certification:

- Best Practice Guidelines: Developing and disseminating best practice guidelines and standards for restorative justice practitioners ensures consistency and quality across programs.

- Certification Programs: Implementing certification programs for restorative justice practitioners enhances professional standards and credibility.

Expanding the Reach of Restorative Justice

Innovations in practice are expanding the reach of restorative justice, making it accessible to a wider range of individuals and communities.

1. Community-Based Initiatives:

1. Grassroots Movements:

- Community-Led Programs: Supporting grassroots movements and community-led restorative justice programs empowers communities to address conflicts and build resilience.

- Local Leadership: Developing local leadership in restorative justice promotes sustainability and ensures that programs are culturally relevant and responsive to community needs.

2. Partnerships and Collaborations:

- Cross-Sector Partnerships: Building partnerships with various sectors, including education, healthcare, and social services, enhances the reach and impact of restorative justice programs.

- Collaborative Networks: Creating collaborative networks of restorative justice practitioners and organizations fosters knowledge sharing, innovation, and mutual support.

2. Policy and Advocacy:

1. Legislative Support:

- Policy Advocacy: Advocating for policies and legislation that support the integration of restorative justice into the criminal justice system and other sectors promotes systemic change.

- Funding and Resources: Securing funding and resources through policy initiatives ensures the sustainability and expansion of restorative justice programs.

2. Public Awareness:

- Education Campaigns: Conducting public education campaigns to raise awareness about the benefits of restorative justice and its potential to address a wide range of conflicts.

- Media Engagement: Utilizing media to highlight success stories and positive outcomes of restorative justice programs, building public support and understanding.

Case Study: Innovative Restorative Justice Program

Background:

- A community-based restorative justice program in a large urban area aimed to address youth violence and promote community healing through innovative practices.

Innovations and Approaches:

1. Virtual Mediation:

- Online Platforms: The program utilized virtual mediation platforms to engage youth, victims, and community members in restorative processes, overcoming geographical and logistical barriers.

- Digital Resources: Digital tools and resources were provided to participants, including educational videos, mediation guides, and support materials.

2. Trauma-Informed Practices:

- Holistic Support: The program integrated trauma-informed practices, offering counseling and support services to address the underlying trauma contributing to youth violence.

- Safe Spaces: Creating safe spaces for dialogue and healing, both online and in-person, ensured that participants felt supported and respected.

3. Community Circles:

- Inclusive Participation: Community circles involved a wide range of stakeholders, including youth, families, educators, law enforcement, and local leaders, fostering collective problem-solving and community cohesion.

- Cultural Relevance: The program incorporated culturally relevant practices and rituals to ensure that restorative processes resonated with the diverse community.

Outcomes:

- Reduced Youth Violence: The program achieved a significant reduction in youth violence and recidivism rates, contributing to a safer community.

- Enhanced Community Cohesion: Community circles and inclusive participation strengthened community bonds and promoted a culture of mutual support and accountability.

- Policy Influence: The program's success influenced local policymakers to support the expansion of restorative justice initiatives and integrate restorative practices into youth justice policies.

Conclusion

Innovations in restorative justice practice are continuously emerging, driven by research, technology, and evolving societal needs. These innovations, including technological advancements, new approaches, and methodological improvements, enhance the impact and reach of restorative justice. By embracing these innovations, practitioners can address a wider range of conflicts, promote healing and reconciliation, and build more resilient and cohesive communities. As restorative justice continues to evolve, ongoing innovation and adaptation will be essential for meeting the changing needs of individuals and communities and promoting a more just and compassionate society.

Future Directions in Restorative Justice

Expanding Applications Beyond Criminal Justice

Restorative justice principles and practices have traditionally been associated with the criminal justice system, focusing on healing and reconciliation between victims and offenders. However, these principles can be applied beyond criminal justice to foster a culture of peace, empathy, and reconciliation across various sectors of society. This chapter explores the expanding applications of restorative justice in schools, workplaces, and communities, highlighting the benefits and implementation strategies for each context.

Restorative Justice in Schools

Applying restorative justice in schools can significantly impact the educational environment by addressing conflicts, promoting positive behavior, and fostering a supportive school culture.

1. Addressing Conflicts:

1. Peer Mediation:

- Student Mediators: Training students to act as peer mediators empowers them to resolve conflicts among their peers constructively.

- Conflict Resolution Skills: Peer mediation programs teach students valuable conflict resolution skills, promoting peaceful interactions and reducing disciplinary issues.

2. Restorative Circles:

- Dialogue Circles: Implementing restorative circles allows students to engage in open dialogue, share their perspectives, and collaboratively address conflicts.

- Inclusive Participation: Restorative circles involve all affected parties, including students, teachers, and parents, ensuring a comprehensive and inclusive approach to conflict resolution.

2. Promoting Positive Behavior:

1. Restorative Discipline:

- Alternative to Punitive Measures: Restorative discipline focuses on repairing harm and restoring relationships rather than relying solely on punitive measures.

- Behavioral Accountability: Encouraging students to take responsibility for their actions and make amends promotes accountability and behavioral change.

2. Positive Reinforcement:

- Recognition Programs: Implementing programs that recognize and reward positive behavior reinforces a culture of respect and empathy within the school community.

- Behavioral Contracts: Developing behavioral contracts that outline expected behaviors and the consequences of not meeting them helps students understand and adhere to school norms.

3. Fostering a Supportive School Culture:

1. Community Building:

- School-Wide Initiatives: Organizing school-wide initiatives, such as assemblies and workshops, that promote restorative justice principles fosters a sense of community and collective responsibility.

- Mentorship Programs: Establishing mentorship programs that pair older students with younger ones provides guidance, support, and positive role models.

2. Teacher Training:

- Restorative Practices Training: Providing teachers with training in restorative practices equips them with the skills to manage classroom conflicts and support students effectively.

- Professional Development: Ongoing professional development opportunities ensure that teachers stay updated on best practices and emerging trends in restorative justice.

Restorative Justice in Workplaces

Implementing restorative justice in workplaces can improve employee relationships, enhance communication, and create a more inclusive and harmonious work environment.

1. Conflict Resolution:

1. Workplace Mediation:

- Professional Mediators: Employing professional mediators to facilitate the resolution of workplace conflicts ensures that disputes are handled impartially and constructively.

- Peer Mediation Programs: Training employees to act as peer mediators empowers them to address conflicts among colleagues effectively.

2. Restorative Circles:

- Dialogue Circles: Implementing restorative circles in the workplace allows employees to engage in open dialogue, share their concerns, and collaboratively resolve conflicts.

- Team Building: Restorative circles can also be used for team-building activities, fostering trust and cooperation among team members.

2. Enhancing Communication:

1. Open Communication Channels:

- Feedback Systems: Establishing formal feedback systems that encourage open communication and constructive feedback promotes transparency and trust.

- Suggestion Boxes: Providing anonymous suggestion boxes allows employees to voice their concerns and suggestions without fear of retaliation.

2. Training Programs:

- Communication Skills Training: Offering training programs that focus on active listening, empathy, and effective communication enhances interpersonal relationships and reduces misunderstandings.

- Conflict Resolution Workshops: Conducting workshops on conflict resolution strategies equips employees with the skills to manage and resolve conflicts independently.

3. Creating an Inclusive Work Environment:

1. Diversity and Inclusion Initiatives:

- Cultural Competency Training: Providing cultural competency training ensures that employees understand and respect diverse perspectives and backgrounds.

- Diversity Committees: Establishing diversity committees that promote inclusive practices and address issues related to discrimination and bias fosters an inclusive work environment.

2. Restorative Policies:

- Restorative HR Policies: Developing HR policies that incorporate restorative justice principles, such as fair disciplinary procedures and support for conflict resolution, ensures a just and equitable workplace.

- Employee Assistance Programs: Offering employee assistance programs that provide support for personal and professional challenges promotes employee well-being and productivity.

Restorative Justice in Communities

Applying restorative justice in communities can address social issues, promote community cohesion, and build a culture of mutual support and accountability.

1. Addressing Social Issues:

1. Community Mediation:

- Local Mediators: Training local mediators to facilitate the resolution of community disputes ensures that conflicts are addressed by individuals who understand the community's dynamics.

- Restorative Justice Centers: Establishing restorative justice centers that offer mediation services and support for conflict resolution promotes accessible and effective interventions.

2. Restorative Practices in Housing:

- Tenant-Landlord Mediation: Implementing mediation programs for tenant-landlord disputes ensures that conflicts related to housing are resolved fairly and constructively.

- Neighborhood Dispute Resolution: Offering mediation services for neighborhood disputes, such as noise complaints and property issues, fosters a sense of community and cooperation.

2. Promoting Community Cohesion:

1. Community Circles:

- Dialogue Circles: Organizing community circles that bring together diverse community members to discuss common issues, share experiences, and develop collaborative solutions promotes understanding and unity.

- Healing Circles: Facilitating healing circles that address the impact of community trauma and violence fosters collective healing and resilience.

2. Restorative Community Programs:

- Youth Programs: Developing restorative justice programs for youth, such as mentorship and peer mediation, empowers young people to contribute positively to their communities.

- Elder Mediation: Offering mediation services that address conflicts involving elderly community members ensures that their needs and perspectives are respected and addressed.

3. Building a Culture of Mutual Support and Accountability:

1. Community Initiatives:

- Volunteer Programs: Encouraging community members to participate in volunteer programs that support restorative justice initiatives fosters a sense of collective responsibility and engagement.

- Community Gardens: Establishing community gardens that bring together diverse community members to work collaboratively promotes social cohesion and mutual support.

2. Restorative Policies:

- Restorative City Policies: Advocating for city policies that support the implementation of restorative justice practices in various sectors, such as education, housing, and law enforcement, promotes systemic change.

- Restorative Budgeting: Encouraging participatory budgeting processes that involve community members in decision-making ensures that resources are allocated fairly and equitably.

Benefits of Expanding Restorative Justice Applications

Expanding the applications of restorative justice beyond the criminal justice system offers numerous benefits for individuals, organizations, and communities.

1. Individual Benefits:

- Personal Growth: Participation in restorative justice processes promotes personal growth, accountability, and empathy.

- Emotional Healing: Restorative practices provide opportunities for emotional healing and closure for those affected by conflicts.

2. Organizational Benefits:

- Improved Relationships: Implementing restorative justice in organizations enhances employee relationships, communication, and collaboration.

- Increased Productivity: A positive and inclusive work environment contributes to increased employee well-being and productivity.

3. Community Benefits:

- Social Cohesion: Restorative justice promotes social cohesion by addressing conflicts constructively and fostering a sense of community.

- Collective Empowerment: Community-based restorative practices empower individuals and groups to take an active role in resolving conflicts and promoting justice.

Case Study: Restorative Justice in a School Setting

Background:

- A high school implemented a restorative justice program to address conflicts, reduce disciplinary issues, and promote a positive school culture.

Implementation Strategies:

1. Peer Mediation Program:

- Training Students: Selected students were trained as peer mediators to help resolve conflicts among their peers.

- Mediation Sessions: Peer mediators conducted mediation sessions during school hours, providing a safe space for students to address their conflicts.

2. Restorative Circles:

- Dialogue Circles: Restorative circles were held regularly to allow students, teachers, and parents to discuss issues and collaboratively develop solutions.

- Support Circles: Support circles were organized for students facing personal challenges, providing emotional and peer support.

3. Teacher Training:

- Professional Development: Teachers received training in restorative practices, equipping them with the skills to manage classroom conflicts and support students effectively.

Outcomes:

1. Reduced Disciplinary Issues:

- Lower Suspension Rates: The school observed a significant reduction in suspension rates, as conflicts were resolved through restorative practices rather than punitive measures.

- Improved Behavior: Students demonstrated improved behavior and accountability, contributing to a positive school environment.

2. Enhanced School Culture:

- Increased Empathy: Participation in restorative circles and peer mediation programs fostered empathy and understanding among students.

- Stronger Community: The school community became more cohesive and supportive, with students, teachers, and parents working together to promote a positive culture.

Conclusion

Expanding the applications of restorative justice beyond the criminal justice system offers significant benefits for schools, workplaces, and communities. By addressing conflicts, promoting positive behavior, and fostering a culture of peace, empathy, and reconciliation, restorative justice principles can transform various sectors of society. Implementing restorative practices in diverse contexts requires strategic planning, training, and community engagement, but the rewards of a more just and compassionate society are well worth the effort. Through continuous innovation and adaptation, restorative justice can continue to grow and positively impact individuals, organizations, and communities worldwide.

Vision for a Restorative Society

Envisioning a restorative society involves imagining a world where restorative justice principles guide our responses to conflict and harm. This vision encompasses systemic changes, cultural shifts, and the collective commitment to healing, justice, and reconciliation. By integrating restorative practices into various facets of society, we can build communities that prioritize empathy, accountability, and mutual support. This chapter explores the key components of a restorative society, the steps needed to achieve this vision, and the transformative impact such a society could have.

Key Components of a Restorative Society

A restorative society is built on principles that promote healing, justice, and reconciliation across all sectors. The following components are essential for creating and sustaining a restorative society:

1. Systemic Integration of Restorative Practices:

1. Criminal Justice System:

- Restorative Alternatives: Implementing restorative alternatives to traditional punitive measures, such as mediation, circles, and conferencing, to address crimes and conflicts.

- Rehabilitation and Reentry: Focusing on the rehabilitation and reintegration of offenders into society through restorative practices that promote accountability and personal growth.

2. Educational Institutions:

- Restorative Discipline: Adopting restorative approaches to discipline that focus on repairing harm and restoring relationships rather than punitive measures.

- Inclusive Practices: Integrating restorative practices into the curriculum and school culture to promote a positive and inclusive learning environment.

3. Workplaces:

- Conflict Resolution: Implementing restorative processes to address workplace conflicts, improve communication, and build a collaborative work culture.

- Employee Well-Being: Prioritizing employee well-being through restorative practices that support mental health, inclusivity, and work-life balance.

4. Community Organizations:

- Community Engagement: Encouraging community participation in restorative justice initiatives to address local conflicts and promote social cohesion.

- Support Systems: Establishing support systems for individuals affected by harm, including victims, offenders, and their families.

2. Cultural Shifts Towards Restorative Values:

1. Empathy and Compassion:

- Cultural Norms: Promoting empathy and compassion as cultural norms, encouraging individuals to understand and support one another.

- Education and Awareness: Educating the public about the importance of empathy and compassion in fostering a restorative society.

2. Accountability and Responsibility:

- Personal Accountability: Encouraging individuals to take responsibility for their actions and make amends for any harm caused.

- Collective Responsibility: Promoting a sense of collective responsibility, where communities work together to address and prevent harm.

3. Healing and Reconciliation:

- Healing Processes: Integrating healing processes into responses to conflict and harm, prioritizing the emotional and psychological well-being of all parties involved.

- Reconciliation Efforts: Facilitating reconciliation efforts that aim to restore relationships and rebuild trust within communities.

3. Commitment to Social Justice and Equity:

1. Inclusive Policies:

- Equitable Access: Ensuring that restorative justice practices are accessible to all individuals, regardless of socioeconomic status, race, gender, or other identities.

- Anti-Discrimination: Implementing policies that actively combat discrimination and promote equity and inclusion.

2. Community Empowerment:

- Participatory Decision-Making: Encouraging participatory decision-making processes that involve community members in shaping policies and practices.

- Grassroots Movements: Supporting grassroots movements that advocate for social justice and the implementation of restorative practices.

3. Systemic Change:

- Policy Reform: Advocating for policy reforms that integrate restorative justice principles into various sectors, including criminal justice, education, and healthcare.

- Sustainable Practices: Promoting sustainable practices that address the root causes of harm and support long-term social change.

Steps to Achieve a Restorative Society

Achieving a restorative society requires a concerted effort from individuals, communities, organizations, and policymakers. The following steps outline the pathway to realizing this vision:

1. Education and Advocacy:

1. Public Awareness Campaigns:

- Media Engagement: Utilizing media platforms to raise awareness about restorative justice principles and their benefits.

- Community Outreach: Conducting community outreach programs to educate the public about restorative practices and how they can be involved.

2. Policy Advocacy:

- Legislative Action: Advocating for legislative changes that support the integration of restorative justice into the criminal justice system and other sectors.

- Collaborative Efforts: Building coalitions and networks of advocates to amplify the call for restorative justice policy reforms.

2. Capacity Building and Training:

1. Professional Development:

- Training Programs: Offering comprehensive training programs for professionals in various fields, including law enforcement, education, and social services.

- Continuous Learning: Encouraging continuous professional development to keep practitioners updated on best practices and emerging trends.

2. Community Training:

- Restorative Workshops: Conducting workshops and seminars for community members to learn about restorative justice and how to implement it in their daily lives.

- Peer Mediation Programs: Establishing peer mediation programs that empower individuals to resolve conflicts within their communities.

3. Implementation and Evaluation:

1. Pilot Programs:

- Testing Innovations: Implementing pilot programs to test new restorative practices and approaches in various settings.

- Monitoring Outcomes: Monitoring and evaluating the outcomes of pilot programs to identify best practices and areas for improvement.

2. Scalability:

- Expanding Successful Models: Scaling up successful pilot programs to reach a broader population and integrate restorative practices more widely.

- Adapting to Contexts: Adapting restorative practices to fit different cultural and organizational contexts, ensuring relevance and effectiveness.

4. Building Collaborative Partnerships:

1. Cross-Sector Collaboration:

- Interdisciplinary Teams: Forming interdisciplinary teams that bring together professionals from various fields to collaborate on restorative justice initiatives.

- Shared Resources: Sharing resources, knowledge, and expertise across sectors to enhance the impact of restorative practices.

2. Community Partnerships:

- Local Organizations: Partnering with local organizations to implement restorative justice initiatives that address specific community needs.

- Volunteer Networks: Establishing volunteer networks that support restorative justice programs and promote community involvement.

Transformative Impact of a Restorative Society

A restorative society has the potential to transform the way we address conflict and harm, leading to numerous positive outcomes for individuals and communities:

1. Reduced Recidivism and Crime Rates:

- Rehabilitation Focus: Prioritizing rehabilitation and reintegration reduces recidivism rates and promotes long-term public safety.

- Preventive Measures: Addressing the root causes of harm through restorative practices prevents future conflicts and criminal behavior.

2. Enhanced Community Cohesion:

- Strong Relationships: Building strong, trust-based relationships within communities fosters social cohesion and collective resilience.

- Mutual Support: Promoting mutual support and accountability strengthens the social fabric and empowers communities to address challenges collaboratively.

3. Improved Mental and Emotional Well-Being:

- Healing Processes: Providing opportunities for healing and reconciliation enhances the mental and emotional well-being of individuals affected by harm.

- Support Systems: Establishing support systems for victims, offenders, and their families promotes holistic well-being and recovery.

4. Social Justice and Equity:

- Inclusive Practices: Ensuring that restorative practices are inclusive and accessible promotes social justice and addresses systemic inequalities.

- Empowered Communities: Empowering communities to take an active role in justice processes fosters equity and supports marginalized groups.

Case Study: A Restorative Society in Action

Background:

- A mid-sized city implemented a comprehensive restorative justice initiative aimed at transforming its approach to conflict and harm across various sectors, including criminal justice, education, and community services.

Implementation Strategies:

1. Criminal Justice System:

- Restorative Diversion Programs: The city established diversion programs that referred eligible offenders to restorative justice processes instead of traditional court proceedings.

- Reentry Support: Restorative reentry programs provided support for formerly incarcerated individuals, including mediation, counseling, and job training.

2. Educational Institutions:

- Restorative Schools Initiative: The city launched an initiative to integrate restorative practices into all public schools, focusing on peer mediation, restorative discipline, and community-building activities.

- Teacher Training: Teachers received extensive training in restorative practices, equipping them to manage classroom conflicts and support students effectively.

3. Community Engagement:

- Community Circles: Regular community circles were held to address local conflicts, promote dialogue, and foster social cohesion.

- Volunteer Programs: A network of trained volunteers supported restorative justice initiatives, providing mediation services and facilitating restorative circles.

Outcomes:

1. Reduced Recidivism:

- Lower Rates: The city observed a significant reduction in recidivism rates among offenders who participated in restorative justice programs compared to those in traditional court processes.

- Positive Behavioral Change: Offenders demonstrated sustained positive behavioral changes, contributing to long-term public safety.

2. Improved School Climate:

- Decreased Disciplinary Issues: Schools reported a decrease in disciplinary issues, suspensions, and expulsions, as conflicts were resolved through restorative practices.

- Enhanced Student Well-Being: Students experienced improved mental and emotional well-being, feeling supported and understood within the school community.

3. Strengthened Community Bonds:

- Increased Trust: Community circles and restorative practices fostered trust and cooperation among community members, enhancing social cohesion.

- Collective Empowerment: The initiative empowered community members to take an active role in addressing conflicts

CONCLUSION

SUMMARIZING KEY INSIGHTS

The journey through the principles, processes, and impact of victim-offender mediation highlights its transformative potential. Restorative justice offers a holistic and humane approach to addressing harm, promoting healing, and fostering reconciliation. This conclusion chapter synthesizes the key insights from our exploration, emphasizing the essential elements of restorative justice, the benefits it offers, and the vision for a restorative society.

Core Principles of Restorative Justice

Restorative justice is grounded in principles that prioritize healing, accountability, and community involvement. The core principles include:

1. Repairing Harm:

- Focus on Victims: Restorative justice centers the needs and experiences of victims, providing them with a platform to voice their pain, seek answers, and participate in the justice process.

- Reparation: Offenders are encouraged to take responsibility for their actions and make amends, promoting genuine accountability and reparative actions.

2. Inclusive Dialogue:

- Stakeholder Engagement: Involving all affected parties—victims, offenders, families, and community members—ensures that diverse perspectives are considered and respected.

- Collaborative Problem-Solving: Facilitated dialogue allows participants to collaboratively develop solutions and agreements that address the harm and promote healing.

3. Reintegration:

- Supportive Processes: Restorative justice supports the reintegration of offenders into society by addressing underlying issues and fostering personal growth.

- Community Building: The approach strengthens community ties and promotes a culture of mutual support and accountability.

Key Processes in Victim-Offender Mediation

Victim-offender mediation is a pivotal process within the restorative justice framework, involving several critical steps:

1. Preparation and Assessment:

- Screening for Suitability: Ensuring that both victims and offenders are suitable and willing participants is crucial for a successful mediation.

- Informed Consent: Participants must be fully informed about the process and give their voluntary consent to participate.

2. Mediation Session:

- Facilitated Dialogue: Trained mediators guide the conversation, ensuring that it remains respectful and constructive, allowing participants to express their feelings and perspectives.

- Agreement Development: The goal is to reach a mutually acceptable agreement that addresses the harm and outlines steps for reparation and reconciliation.

3. Follow-Up and Implementation:

- Monitoring Agreements: Ensuring that the agreed-upon actions are implemented and supporting participants throughout the process is vital for long-term success.

- Continued Support: Providing ongoing resources and support to both victims and offenders helps sustain the positive outcomes of the mediation.

Impact and Benefits of Restorative Justice

The impact of restorative justice extends beyond the immediate resolution of conflicts, offering numerous long-term benefits:

1. Healing and Empowerment:

- For Victims: Victims gain a sense of empowerment and closure by having their voices heard and their needs addressed.

- For Offenders: Offenders experience personal growth and rehabilitation through accountability and the opportunity to make amends.

2. Community Strengthening:

- Social Cohesion: Restorative justice fosters stronger community bonds by promoting empathy, respect, and collective responsibility.

- Reduced Recidivism: By addressing the root causes of harmful behavior, restorative justice reduces recidivism rates and promotes lasting change.

3. Systemic Change:

- Transformative Potential: Restorative justice has the potential to transform traditional justice systems by offering more humane and effective responses to conflict and harm.

- Policy and Practice Integration: Integrating restorative practices into various sectors, such as education, workplaces, and communities, promote a culture of peace and reconciliation.

Vision for a Restorative Society

Envisioning a restorative society involves imagining a world where restorative justice principles guide our responses to conflict and harm. This vision includes:

1. Systemic Integration:

- Criminal Justice: Implementing restorative alternatives within the criminal justice system focuses on rehabilitation and reconciliation rather than punishment.

- Education and Workplaces: Adopting restorative practices in schools and workplaces promotes positive behavior, conflict resolution, and a supportive culture.

2. Cultural Shifts:

- Empathy and Compassion: Promoting empathy and compassion as cultural norms encourages understanding and support within communities.

- Accountability and Responsibility: Emphasizing personal and collective accountability fosters a sense of shared responsibility for addressing harm.

3. Commitment to Equity:

- Inclusive Practices: Ensuring that restorative justice practices are accessible and equitable addresses systemic inequalities and promotes social justice.

- Community Empowerment: Empowering communities to take an active role in justice processes supports marginalized groups and fosters collective resilience.

Achieving a Restorative Society

Achieving a restorative society requires a coordinated effort involving education, advocacy, capacity building, and collaboration:

1. Education and Advocacy:

- Raising Awareness: Public awareness campaigns and community outreach programs educate the public about restorative justice principles and benefits.

- Policy Advocacy: Advocating for legislative changes supports the integration of restorative justice into various sectors.

2. Capacity Building and Training:

- Professional Development: Offering training programs for professionals ensures that they are equipped with the skills to implement restorative practices effectively.

- Community Training: Conducting workshops for community members empowers them to resolve conflicts and promote restorative principles.

3. Implementation and Evaluation:

- Pilot Programs: Implementing pilot programs allows for testing and refining new approaches before scaling up.

- Monitoring and Evaluation: Regular evaluation ensures continuous improvement and adaptation to changing needs.

4. Building Collaborative Partnerships:

- Cross-Sector Collaboration: Forming interdisciplinary teams and collaborative networks enhances the impact of restorative justice initiatives.

- Community Partnerships: Partnering with local organizations and establishing volunteer networks promotes community involvement and support.

Conclusion

Restorative justice represents a profound shift in how we address conflict and harm, offering a more humane, effective, and inclusive approach. By embracing the principles of repairing harm, inclusive dialogue, and reintegration, we can foster healing, accountability, and reconciliation. The journey through victim-offender mediation and the broader application of restorative justice practices highlights their transformative potential for individuals, communities, and society as a whole.

As we envision and work toward a restorative society, we must remain committed to education, advocacy, and collaboration. By integrating restorative practices into various sectors and promoting cultural shifts towards empathy, compassion, and accountability, we can build a more just and compassionate world. The vision of a restorative society is not only possible but within our reach, offering hope and healing for future generations.

Call to Action for Stakeholders

Stakeholders, including policymakers, practitioners, and community members, are called to support and advocate for restorative justice. Collective efforts are essential to integrate restorative practices into our justice systems and communities, ensuring their sustainability and effectiveness. This call to action outlines the specific roles and responsibilities of various stakeholders in promoting and advancing restorative justice.

Policymakers

Policymakers play a critical role in shaping the legislative and policy framework that supports restorative justice. Their commitment and action are vital for the integration and expansion of restorative practices.

1. Legislative Advocacy:

- Enact Supportive Laws: Advocate for and enact laws that formally recognize and support restorative justice practices within the criminal justice system, education, and other sectors.

- Allocate Funding: Ensure adequate funding and resources are allocated to develop, implement, and sustain restorative justice programs.

2. Policy Development:

- Create Comprehensive Policies: Develop comprehensive policies that integrate restorative justice principles into various sectors, including criminal justice, education, and social services.

- Support Research and Evaluation: Fund and support research and evaluation efforts to build a robust evidence base for restorative justice practices and their outcomes.

3. Public Awareness:

- Raise Awareness: Use your platform to raise public awareness about the benefits and effectiveness of restorative justice, fostering community support and engagement.

- Engage Stakeholders: Facilitate dialogue and collaboration among diverse stakeholders, including justice professionals, educators, community leaders, and victims' advocates.

Practitioners

Practitioners, including mediators, educators, social workers, and law enforcement officers, are at the forefront of implementing restorative justice practices. Their expertise and commitment are crucial for the success of restorative initiatives.

1. Professional Development:

- Pursue Training: Engage in continuous professional development and training to stay updated on best practices and emerging trends in restorative justice.

- Mentor and Train Others: Mentor and train new practitioners, sharing knowledge and skills to build a strong network of restorative justice professionals.

2. Implement Restorative Practices:

- Integrate into Work: Integrate restorative practices into your daily work, whether in criminal justice, schools, workplaces, or community organizations.

- Facilitate Processes: Facilitate restorative justice processes with empathy, impartiality, and a commitment to healing and reconciliation.

3. Advocate for Change:

- Promote Restorative Justice: Advocate for the adoption and expansion of restorative justice practices within your professional community and beyond.

- Share Success Stories: Share success stories and evidence of the positive impact of restorative justice to build support and credibility.

Community Members

Community members play a vital role in supporting and sustaining restorative justice practices. Their involvement and commitment can drive grassroots initiatives and foster a culture of empathy and accountability.

1. Engage in Restorative Practices:

- Participate Actively: Actively participate in restorative justice processes, such as community circles, peer mediation, and local restorative justice programs.

- Support Victims and Offenders: Offer support to both victims and offenders, helping them navigate the restorative justice process and promoting healing.

2. Advocate for Restorative Justice:

- Raise Awareness: Raise awareness about the benefits of restorative justice within your community, encouraging others to learn about and support restorative practices.

- Organize Initiatives: Organize community initiatives that promote restorative justice, such as workshops, seminars, and public discussions.

3. Foster a Restorative Culture:

- Promote Empathy and Compassion: Promote empathy, compassion, and mutual support within your community, creating an environment where restorative practices can thrive.

- Build Networks: Build networks and partnerships with local organizations, schools, and justice professionals to support the implementation and sustainability of restorative justice programs.

Conclusion

The journey toward a restorative society requires the collective efforts of all stakeholders. Policymakers, practitioners, and community members each have a unique and essential role to play in promoting and advancing restorative justice. By working together, we can integrate restorative practices into our justice systems and communities, ensuring their sustainability and effectiveness.

This call to action invites you to join the movement for restorative justice, advocate for change, implement restorative practices, and foster a culture of empathy, accountability, and healing. Together, we can build a more just and compassionate society, where restorative justice principles guide our responses to conflict and harm, and where every individual and community can thrive.

Envisioning a Restorative Future

A restorative future is one where justice is not merely punitive but also healing and transformative. By embracing restorative justice, we can build societies that prioritize empathy, accountability, and the collective well-being of all members. This vision for a restorative future encompasses a holistic approach to addressing conflict and harm, creating communities where everyone feels valued, supported, and empowered.

Embracing Empathy and Compassion

1. Centering Empathy in Justice:

- Understanding Experiences: In a restorative future, justice systems center the experiences and needs of victims, providing them with opportunities to be heard, understood, and supported.

- Building Connections: Offenders are encouraged to understand the impact of their actions, fostering empathy and genuine remorse, and leading to meaningful reconciliation.

2. Promoting Compassionate Communities:

- Community Support: Communities are built on principles of compassion and mutual support, where individuals look out for one another and work together to address harm and prevent future conflicts.

- Inclusive Practices: Compassionate communities are inclusive, ensuring that all members, regardless of background, are valued and have access to restorative justice processes.

Fostering Accountability and Responsibility

1. Encouraging Personal Accountability:

- Taking Responsibility: Offenders are encouraged to take responsibility for their actions, understanding the harm caused and committing to making amends.

- Restorative Agreements: Through restorative agreements, offenders actively participate in repairing the harm, promoting accountability and personal growth.

2. Cultivating Collective Responsibility:

- Shared Ownership: Communities take shared ownership of addressing and preventing harm, recognizing that everyone has a role in fostering a safe and supportive environment.

- Collaborative Problem-Solving: Collective responsibility involves collaborative problem-solving, where community members work together to find solutions and support one another in the healing process.

Promoting Healing and Transformation

1. Healing-Centered Justice:

- Focus on Healing: Justice processes prioritize healing for all parties involved, addressing emotional and psychological needs and promoting holistic well-being.

- Support Systems: Comprehensive support systems are in place to assist victims, offenders, and their families throughout the restorative process.

2. Transformative Practices:

- Personal Transformation: Restorative justice encourages personal transformation for offenders, providing opportunities for rehabilitation, education, and personal development.

- Community Transformation: Communities transform through the collective healing process, becoming more resilient, cohesive, and equipped to handle future conflicts constructively.

Building Sustainable and Resilient Societies

1. Integrating Restorative Practices:

- Systemic Integration: Restorative practices are integrated into all sectors of society, including criminal justice, education, workplaces, and community organizations, ensuring a consistent and supportive approach to addressing harm.

- Policy and Legislation: Supportive policies and legislation create a framework for the sustainable implementation and expansion of restorative justice programs.

2. Fostering a Culture of Peace:

- Peaceful Conflict Resolution: Societies prioritize peaceful conflict resolution, using restorative practices to address disputes and promote harmony.

- Preventive Measures: Preventive measures, such as education and community-building activities, are in place to reduce the occurrence of conflicts and promote a culture of peace.

Conclusion

Envisioning a restorative future involves reimagining justice as a healing and transformative process. By embracing restorative justice principles, we can build societies that prioritize empathy, accountability, and the collective well-being of all members. This vision calls for the integration of restorative practices into various sectors, fostering compassionate communities, and promoting healing and transformation for individuals and communities alike.

In a restorative future, justice systems, educational institutions, workplaces, and community organizations work together to address harm constructively and supportively. Through collective efforts and a commitment to restorative principles, we can create a more just and compassionate world, where everyone has the opportunity to heal, grow, and thrive.